learning to talk sheep

LEARNING TO TALK SHEEP

Understanding Those You Lead

C. Wayne Perry and
Christopher W. Perry

THE PILGRIM PRESS
CLEVELAND

WE *dedicate this book to our wonderful wives, Donna and Renae. They have taught us more about relationships than all the courses, workshops, and research we have done put together because they have revealed all our flaws and loved us anyway.*

The Pilgrim Press, 700 Prospect Avenue, Cleveland, Ohio 44115
thepilgrimpress.com

Printed in the United States of America on acid-free paper

14 13 12 11 10 5 4 3 2

Library of Congress Cataloging-in-Publication Data

Perry, C. Wayne, 1948–
Learning to talk sheep : understanding those you lead / by C. Wayne Perry and Christopher W. Perry.
p. cm.
Includes bibliographical references (p.).
ISBN 978-0-8298-1850-5 (alk. paper)
1. Pastoral theology. 2. Typology (Psychology)—Religious aspects—Christianity. I. Perry, Christopher W., 1974– II. Title.
BV4011.3.P47 2010
259—dc22 2010002564

Contents

Acknowledgments

Wayne would like to thank:

— The many hundreds of people I have had the privilege of knowing and serving, both as a minister and as a therapist. Each of these people has touched my life in some way. Each of these has been a "living human document" who taught me more of what it means to be a shepherd to God's sheep. Without them, this book would be just theory. They are the crucible in which the theory has been tried, refined, and tested.

— Dr. Terry Gunnells, Rev. Joe James Peterson, Ms. Carole Power, and Dr. John Mark Trent, who took the time to help read through parts of the original manuscript and provide feedback. This book is partially a result of their two-way communication.

Chris would like to thank:

— My boys, Caleb and Cole, for putting up with the time I had to spend writing when they would rather have had me playing with them (and thanks, Mom, for being such a good babysitter!).

— The people of Robinson Springs United Methodist Church for granting me the time and support needed to work on this project and for at least pretending to be interested when I rambled on about all the theories we were writing about.

— My dad. Not every son gets to coauthor a book with his father. Thanks, Dad, for the original idea and trusting me enough with your ideas to make this book work.

— Kim Martin Sadler, Joan Blake, and the folks at The Pilgrim Press for all of your help and for taking a chance on our idea.

Introduction: WHY SHEEP?

Without a shepherd,
sheep are not a flock.

—RUSSIAN PROVERB

It seems any time leaders gather, especially at conferences, a favorite pastime is to break out the "war stories." It almost seems to turn into a game of one-upsmanship to see who has the craziest coworker or church member. Your colleagues will laugh with you, maybe give you some advice, good or otherwise, and then share their own stories. To listen to these leaders talk, one could easily draw the conclusion that our churches and workplaces are full of crazy, stubborn, vindictive, or dumb people. The fact is, however, that your flock may be talking about you the same way when they gather.

Actually, if we are honest, we will recognize that the people of our workplaces and churches are mostly intelligent, normal people. Why, then, do they drive many of us in leadership a little batty?

The biggest reason is our inability as leaders to properly understand the motivations and behaviors of those who are our followers. This book seeks to address that issue.

Before we dive directly into the topic, we must first make some crucial definitions. First, we hope that this book is useful for all leaders, regardless of occupation. Please recognize, however, that this book is written from the perspective of religious professionals. Wayne comes to this book as one who has been an ordained pastor for more than thirty years, twenty-three of those spent as a U.S. Air Force chaplain. He also has many years of experience as a marriage and family therapist and has served as a consultant on organizational development to both military and civilian organizations. Chris has been in ministry for fifteen years and has served in a variety of contexts—large churches, small churches, rural and urban, new (church planting) and old (he has served churches dating to 1812 and 1828). He has also committed himself to the study of the best in leadership. Through his doctoral work he was able to visit the most cutting-edge churches in the country and study with internationally recognized leadership experts in both the church and corporate worlds. In our various experiences we have had the privilege of talking and working with people from a variety of backgrounds.

All of this has taught us that the people described in this book can be found in every organization, no matter how large or small. Therefore, we have tried to make our language as neutral as possible. Even so, we recognize that every organization, especially those of a religious nature, uses a unique language to define its structure. When we refer to a religious body we may be speaking of a church, congregation, synagogue, temple, or mosque. The head of that local body might be called a pastor, preacher, priest, minister, elder, rabbi, or imam. To keep matters simple, when we want to speak of a religious context we will simply refer to the "pastor" of the "church." We may also use the term "clergy" to refer to all religious professionals. We explicitly invite those of you from religious traditions where these terms are not dominant, and those of you reading from a nonreligious context, to fill in your own language (for example, "CEO" or "manager" or your "company"). We are deliberately trying to include all of you. Despite the limitations of language, the principles will apply across the board.

We also wish to make explicit an assumption that we bring to this book—that leaders have the same basic needs and show the same basic behavior patterns as their followers. Some religious bodies believe that clergy become ontologically different (that is, they have a different spiritual nature than the rest of us). Likewise, there are some CEOs who seem to feel they are at least right next to God. We, however, do not know of any religious body or corporation that feels their leader ceases to be human, with all the foibles that implies. So, whatever we say about the sheep also applies to the shepherds.

Finally, we need to make a disclaimer. Throughout this book we have included illustrative material drawn from real-life experiences. Additionally, we include the experiences shared with us by other pastors and leaders. Even so, none of the case material in this book depicts any actual person, living or dead. Rather, the cases are created as composites of real experiences. If the people presented in this book seem real, and if you think you know them, just attribute that as evidence of the universality of what we are describing.

THE BOOK'S METAPHOR

A leadership book calling our followers "sheep" might, at first blush, seem a little strange. In our age of American individualism we rebel strongly against the notion of being a "sheep." Bill Maher, an American comedian and talk show host, summed up the attitude of the country: "We need more people speaking out. This country is not overrun with rebels and free thinkers. It's overrun with sheep and conformists."[1] Obviously, to Maher to be a sheep is a negative thing. Shock rocker Marilyn Manson, speaking to today's youth, agrees with Maher's assessment: "I fear being a completely acceptable sheep in society."[2]

With such a negative attitude towards the idea of being a sheep in our culture, we felt it necessary to begin the book with an explanation of the concept of sheep and shepherd. First, when we refer to sheep we are not suggesting you view your followers as dumb, placid creatures with no ability to do anything constructive on their own. Nor do we wish to suggest that your followers are there to strictly do what you tell them to.

The sheep metaphor comes out of the authors' context. We are both United Methodist pastors and, thus, approach life from a Christian worldview. The sheep/shepherd relationship is one of the most dominant metaphors for the people of God in the Judeo-Christian tradition. Sometimes this reference comes in terms of our human condition, calling the human race like sheep without a shepherd (1 Kings 22:17), meaning that all of us, like sheep, have wandered off the correct path (Isa. 53:6). Most of the time, however, the sheep/shepherd relationship is presented in a very positive light. In Micah's prophesy, God promises to gather all of God's followers safely together like sheep in their pasture (Micah 2:12). Jesus calls himself the Good Shepherd and promises to lay down his own life for his sheep (followers) (John 10:10–15). Jesus also tells the story of the shepherd who finds each individual sheep so valuable that he is willing to leave ninety-nine in the pasture to search for one that is lost (Luke 15:3–7). The Gospels record Jesus' intense compassion for those around him because they were "like sheep without a shepherd" (Matt. 9:36; Mark 6:34). One of the most famous scriptures, Psalm 23, begins, "The Lord is my shepherd." Many other scriptures refer to God as a shepherd leading the sheep (us) to places of safety and freedom.[3]

You might say, "Of course the Bible talks about sheep and shepherds! That was their primary context two thousand years ago, but you don't see too many of them around today." Good point, but that does not mean the metaphor has lost its power; only that the context must be properly framed. What was the purpose of the shepherd? To watch the sheep's every movement because it was too stupid to care for itself. Micromanagement? Of course not! The shepherd had three basic functions: protect, feed, and lead. As a leader, no matter what field you are in, these are still your primary functions, and thus the shepherd/sheep analogy is very applicable. This also defines what your job is not, for example, petting the sheep. Your followers are not your pets, nor are you to spend all of your time trying to placate every bleat. Keep focused on your primary function.

Your first function as a shepherd/leader is to protect the sheep. Sheep, in general, are not very good at defending themselves. The sheep will be completely overwhelmed against a wolf, bear, lion, dog, or just about any other creature it finds itself matched against. You are not going to find a professional sports team naming itself after common sheep. The sheep depend on the shepherd for protection. In the church and business worlds as well as in life, there are still predators trying to get at your sheep. These can be temptations to take shortcuts in the workplace, bad theology or practices in the church, or any other person or way of thinking that can damage your followers' ability to do their job or interact with society in a healthy manner. You must see the dangers first. Some of these dangers come from the sheep themselves, and much of this book will deal with how to spot those dangers.

Another issue related to protecting sheep is their environment. Not all dangers are related to predators intentionally trying to make a meal out of the sheep. Sometimes just the surroundings of the sheep can create danger. When Chris was in college at Mississippi State University, he had several friends who were studying to be veterinarians. One of the most interesting things he learned from these friends is that a sheep that falls onto its back is stuck. This is not just a situation of inconvenience, but is actually life threatening to the sheep. Gases build up in the sheep's stomach through natural digestion. When on its back, the sheep cannot expel these gases and the sheep will suffocate in just a few hours. The wise shepherd watches the environment for obstacles that could cause the sheep to fall or become stuck in such a situation. A wise leader, similarly, should monitor the environment of the church or workplace to ensure that obstacles are removed. Some obstacles might include lack of resources, lack of training, poor morale, an overly competitive environment, or any numerous other environmental factors that could prevent your followers from achieving their maximum potential.

Your second function is to feed your sheep. In leadership, feeding your flock means you constantly look for helpful ways to encourage each "sheep" to grow to full potential. Let's be honest . . . the vast majority of people are not self-motivated enough to consistently look for ways to challenge their emotional, spiritual, and intellectual lives. In other words, they can't feed themselves. As a shepherd/leader your job is to help your sheep find good food. All sheep want to eat. The innate desire is there, but they need help finding good nourishment, as opposed to chomping down on anything that looks vaguely green.

As you better understand the types of sheep in your flock, you will better understand their nutritional needs. If you do your job properly, you will eventually teach the sheep to find their own food. A good leader works to wean the followers from total dependence. While having others look to you for their every need can be a nice stroke to the ego, it is not in the best interests of your followers. When you teach those around you how to nourish their minds and spirits, they will become much more effective than if they were depending upon you. Actually, as we will discuss in a later chapter, they will become shepherds themselves, thus furthering your influence through those you have led.

Your third function is to lead the flock. If the shepherd doesn't lead, the sheep will either stay put until they starve, or all of them will wander in different directions. Sheep want to respond to the shepherd, but they cannot respond if the shepherd does not lead. As will be discussed throughout this book, different types of sheep need to be led differently. All, however, will follow if the shepherd has a firm and fixed destination and a clear vision that others understand.

Regardless of your context, we hope you find this book helpful—both in understanding the way you function and in understanding how to best lead your sheep. May God grant you the grace to be the shepherd you were called to be.

1

LISTEN TO YOUR FLOCK

Know how to listen
and you will profit even from
those who talk badly.

—PLUTARCH, GREEK HISTORIAN AND PHILOSOPHER

Some years ago, Wayne saw a poster that read: "I know you think you heard what I said, but I am not sure that you know that what I said is not what I meant." Listening should be easy. After all, unless we were born deaf, we came into this world listening to the people around us. There is much evidence that even infants in the womb respond to sound. Spend any time with a deaf person and you will quickly see that they, too, have learned how to "listen" to others using their other senses. Yet one of the most common complaints any leader is likely to hear, especially during times of conflict, is "So-and-So just doesn't listen to me." If listening is so natural, why is it so difficult?

Listening is really a very complex process. You do not simply process sounds, but must also encode (and decode) meaning. Colloquially, we refer to this as "reading between the lines." Unless you learn to read "between the lines" you will not "hear" what is being communicated.[1]

At this point you might be thinking, "I thought this was a book on leadership, not communication theory." Yes, it is, but unless you first learn to listen to your followers you will never be a great leader. Lee Iacocca, former CEO of the Chrysler Corporation, once said, "I only wish I could find an institute that teaches people how to listen. Business people need to listen at least as much as they need to talk. Too many people fail to realize that real communication goes in both directions."[2]

Too often leaders assume their followers can clearly "read between the lines" and then are upset when the followers fail to follow what the leader intended for them to accomplish. This also happens in reverse. A subordinate drops hints as to what he or she wants or needs from the boss and then becomes disenchanted and frustrated at work because the boss does not respond to the "hints." Here's how that might look in a relationship setting: Assume that Bob and Sue, two happily married and reasonably intelligent people, have been having a casual conversation. During this discussion, Bob had mentioned that he was feeling highly stressed at work. The conversation continued for several minutes on various topics, and then Sue mentioned she was having problems with her computer and she wanted Bob to work on it so she could e-mail her cousin. Upon hearing that, Bob started yelling, "Can't you see how tired I am? I have to work all day and now you want me to work all night, too!" Sue was hurt. She had no idea where all of that strong emotion came from, and she certainly had not intended to upset Bob.

While human sin is a definite reality, interactions such as Bob and Sue's are most often the result of a failure to "listen between the lines." Both had paid attention to the words, neither was distracted by the television or other obvious hindrances, but neither had accurately "listened between the lines" and therefore both missed something very important. Sue missed how stressed Bob really was because he said it in such a matter-of-fact way. Bob heard Sue's request for help with the computer as "evidence" she did not care a whit for him, only for the work he provided. Their inadvertent misunderstandings made good communication in the future all the more difficult for both of them.

Listening to someone seems so simple. Like Bob and Sue, all of us have been listening our entire lives. We may have even had a course or two in listening skills (a prerequisite for good leadership these days). Most of us understand the basic concepts of listening, such as that we should look at the person speaking and focus our minds on what is being said. Leaders have learned from therapists to repeat back what they have understood the speaker to be saying using the old standby, "So what you're saying is . . ." Yet it is the seeming simplicity that tricks us into thinking we are hearing, when, in fact, we do not really "get it." We may hear the words, but not the message. Jesus understood this reality, which is why he often said, "Let anyone with ears to hear listen" (see, for example, Mark 4:23)! How can we accomplish this seemingly simple task so that we can "get it" when our followers speak to us?

LISTENING TO THE WORDS

It seems self-evident that listening involves verbal communication. Our ears are designed to pick up vibrations in the air created by another person's speech, and to transmit those vibrations to our brain, where they are decoded and turned into "sounds" that we can "hear." That's the technical side of things. As wonderful as this mechanical/biochemical process is, just because you are able to repeat every word someone said at a board meeting does not mean that you "listened" to that person.

The ancient Hebrews believed that to say something, especially to say it in the name of God, was to cause it to come into being. They believed that words have real power—the power to create "reality." That is why, for example, Amaziah, the priest of Bethel, told the prophet Amos to go away and prophesy elsewhere. Amaziah did not want the things Amos was saying to happen, so he told him to go home and say them in Judah, so the things he said would happen there, not in Israel (Amos 6:10–17).

Experientially, we understand this ancient concept. Children sometimes taunt a playmate with insults or slurs. The target of these words may reply, "Sticks and stones may break my bones, but words can never hurt me," which is usually followed by a flood of tears and a mad dash into the sanctuary of home. Words *do* hurt for precisely the reason the ancient Hebrews believed: they create a new reality. When people call us "dumb" or "fat" or "dork" or whatever, those words change our self-perception, and by changing the way we see ourselves, they change the way we interact with others. Words really do create reality.

Unfortunately, we often act as though this were not true. We downplay the importance of words by calling them "just hot air" or other, even less complimentary, phrases. In the midst of an argument we might say something hurtful, then try to minimize the damage by saying, "I was just mad. I didn't mean it." It may very well be true that we do not actually believe the insults we hurl during a verbal battle, but we meant them nevertheless. We unconsciously pick the insults we sling because we know those are the ones that will create the effect we want—they are the ones that will hurt. There is no point insulting someone if he or she doesn't feel hurt.

As a leader, your words are especially powerful. Those who follow you look to your words for guidance, wisdom, definition of who they are, approval, and so on. When you're in a meeting and someone disagrees with you, the way in which you respond to that person will go a long way towards determining your effectiveness as a leader. Do your people feel that you'll listen to them, even if their ideas are different from yours, or do they feel that any public disagreement with you risks humiliation and loss of status? This perception will largely be determined by your ability to read between the lines when your followers speak and to respond appropriately.

Here is the first rule of listening between the lines: Listen to the words that are chosen by the speaker. Although there are some disagreements, most educational research estimates that the average native English speaker has a vocabulary of approximately twenty thousand word families. A word family includes the root word and all of its various forms. For example, "education," "educator," and "educational" comprise one word family. Moreover, due to changes in technology and English usage prompted by television and other popular mass media, the average native English speaker may add as many as one thousand word families each year. Out of all the possible options, which words does the speaker choose? As Mark Twain said, "The difference between the right word and the almost right word is . . . the difference between the lightning bug and the lightning."[3] What impact do those words have on you, the listener?

The second rule of listening between the lines is to listen to your own emotional reaction to the words the speaker used. If you had grown up in a working-class neighborhood in Alabama and one of your friends called out, "Hey, redneck, how ya doin'?" your likely response would be to smile and accept the invitation to play implied in those words. Yet if someone from outside the neighborhood yelled at you, "Hey, redneck . . . ," your immediate reaction would probably be to get ready for a fight. For us Southerners, to be called a "redneck" by anyone except a close friend was a major insult and prompted a strong emotional reaction. As a leader, being aware of such reactions within yourself will allow you to govern your response. When listening, the key for any leader is to respond, not react. Reaction means acting without conscious thought to the stimulus, whether verbal or environmental. A response is acting only through a conscious decision. The ability to respond starts with knowing your emotional triggers and controlling them.

Context gives powerful clues to decoding the meaning of any statement. Words that create feelings of closeness in one context can create animosity in another. An obvious example is the issue of sexual harassment. Words that might engender feelings of closeness when spoken to one's spouse in the privacy of one's own home might engender feelings of profound embarrassment when spoken to the spouse in public where others can hear. On the other hand, they might engender feelings of anger when spoken to a coworker in the workplace. Of course, the same principle applies in nonsexual situations, as the previous example showed.

As transparent as that may seem, it is a major reason why many miscommunications happen. The Greek philosopher Heraclitus said, "You cannot step twice into the same river."[4] In other words, by the time you put your foot into a river, take it out, and put it in again, the river has changed. That is certainly true of our human environments. Not only do we come from different families, different parts of the country, different backgrounds, different religious heritages, and so on, even within the same family and even with identical twins, the experiences of life are different. The context by which words are chosen and interpreted is different. This means, as a leader, you must be very intentional about your word choice and in making sure those words are understood by the listeners. By the same token, make sure you are properly interpreting the words of those speaking to you, keeping in mind your own built-in biases.

Back to the illustration with Bob and Sue: Bob grew up in a family that followed the rule "Men don't complain unless it is really major." Although it was never overtly stated, his father certainly exemplified that rule, as did every male in the family. So Bob spoke his words about being stressed at work out of the context, "If it's important enough for me to mention, she ought to pay attention and know it's very important." Sue, on the other hand, came from a family that valued open and honest sharing of all sorts of information. Her family rule was, "If it's important, tell me so I won't miss it." Sue assumed, from her own context, that if Bob's stress level were that high, he would have said so.

This is where Bob and Sue failed to listen between the lines. When Bob felt discounted by Sue's request for assistance, he could have asked for more information to adequately understand her context. He, might for example, have asked, "Sue, was I not clear that I am feeling very stressed right now and I just need to relax?" As we all know, tone of voice is very important, so the reader will have to supply a sincere and honest, rather than a sarcastic, tone to those words to make this illustration work. Or, if Bob had reacted first, Sue could have steered the communication back on track by saying, "Bob, I'm really puzzled and hurt by the strength of your reaction. Help me to understand. How am I being unfair to you to ask you to do something I know you do so well?"

As Bob and Sue illustrate, rather than assuming you know what the speaker intended, to really listen you have to listen to the impact of the words on you. If the emotional impact does not seem to fit the words (for example, if you believe the insult you feel is unintended), you must, for the sake of clear understanding, communicate your reaction to the speaker. If you are the speaker, your responsibility, then, is to ask the listener how to more accurately say what it is you want to communicate. Again, words create a new reality, for better or worse, and the point of effective communication is to build a shared reality that helps all involved get their needs met. Ideally, each instance of listening between the lines creates a more broadly shared context on which the relationship can build. Leaders have the burden of not only managing their own relationships, but the relationships of all of those under them. If the leader models, and teaches, what effective listening is all about, the entire team/committee/workplace will work together more effectively and be more productive.

As true as all of that is, this is the world after the fall. If there were no sin, communication would work as just described, but that's not reality. When I, the listener, notice that the speaker continues to choose words and phrases that I have already explicitly identified as objectionable or hurtful, I have to assume that we are engaging in an ulterior transaction. That is, I have to assume that the real communication is something other than what the words with their dictionary definitions would indicate.

Most leaders can probably relate to the ulterior transaction idea through the following example of John. John is a manager in his company and is preparing to leave his office for an important meeting. Steve, one of John's coworkers, stops by to talk to John. John listens politely for several minutes, but then, feeling the pressure of his packed schedule, explains he has to go. Steve acknowledges that, but keeps talking. A few minutes later John tries again, a little more firmly, and again, Steve acknowledges his need to go but keeps talking. At this point, John needs to shift his listening from whatever Steve is saying (the surface message) to the ulterior message. In this case, the surface message is whatever Steve is talking about. Steve's ulterior message might be something like, "My issue is more important than your issue." Subsequent chapters in this book will give suggestions for accurately decoding ulterior transactions.

LISTENING TO THE ACTIONS

There is an old saying: "Your actions speak so loud I can't hear a word you're saying." As pastors we are often told, "People would rather see a sermon than hear one." There is real truth in those sayings, yet, even though we all know it, we often act as though they are not true. That is the irony of our miscommunication. On the one hand, we might put too little importance in our words, as the previous section shows. On the other hand, we can also put too much importance in our words, as though our actions do not matter.

To emphasize the importance of making actions match words with teens, Wayne often uses this personal illustration: "In my closet I have a bowling bag. I have a bowling ball with holes personally drilled for me. I have my own bowling shoes. I even have a bowler's towel. That makes me a bowler, right? Well, not actually. You see, I haven't had my bowling bag, my bowling ball, my bowling shoes, or my bowler's towel out of my closet for more than ten years. Even after all these years, I can talk a great game of bowling. My actions, however, do not match my words." The principle is: If you really want to listen between the lines, you have to give equal attention to what I actually say and do.

SPACE SPEAKS

We live in a three-dimensional world, and the way we use the space available to us speaks volumes. In general, the North American culture (other cultures are different) considers the "public zone" to be anything six feet or more from us. We will allow almost anyone in our public zone. You see this at work in a church, social club, or other settings when someone new comes to visit. Current members may greet the newcomer with a handshake, but if you watch closely, one or both parties will often have to lean forward a bit to shake hands. Alternatively, one or both may take a step back from "handshake distance" to give just a little more emotional space. Far from being a bad thing, this is an unconscious recognition that to feel really comfortable in a new situation, we have to keep strangers in our public zone. Indeed, honoring this need is really a form of creating good hospitality. Have you ever had someone you did not know well violate this and come closer than this "public space?" If so, you instantly recognize how uncomfortable that can make you feel.

Our "friendship zone" consists of the area from about six feet to three feet from us. Within this area, we can shake hands comfortably with arms only slightly extended (in contrast to the public zone, where the arm must be nearly fully extended), and we can even put one arm on the other person's shoulders. We are only comfortable with people we know well and trust in the friendship zone. This is why you will see people at gatherings who have known and liked each other for years, standing close together at church suppers or similar events, while newer acquaintances will tend to stand further apart. It has nothing to do with a need for hearing aids. If you are observant, you can tell who really likes whom by simply watching how closely they stand in informal settings. As we will see later in this chapter, that knowledge can prove very useful for any shepherd.

The "intimate zone" is from a few millimeters to about three feet from us. Within this zone, the other person is so close we can only see a very small portion of that person. Within this zone, we can hug, kiss, or embrace the other person. Multiple points of bodily contact are easily possible. Naturally, we are only comfortable having people we truly care about so close to us. Contrary to what commercials would have us believe, it is not about offending someone because our deodorant might not work well or our toothpaste might not have brightened our teeth "enough." When someone is in our intimate zone, they literally and figuratively so fill our field of vision that we cannot see anyone else. We cannot see the approach of any potential dangers. That requires a strong sense of safety, and, for that reason, we will only allow people we really trust within our intimate zone.

The caveat in all of this is human sin. We sometimes allow people into our intimate zone who are not trustworthy, and we sometimes keep people outside our intimate zone who ought to be there (for example, our spouse). The same is true about our other zones. Sin simply means that we do not always choose wisely or appropriately. Yet because we use space so unconsciously, our use of space speaks truth about what we really think and feel, whether our feelings are helpful or not.

There are exceptions that prove the rule that have nothing to do with sin. An elevator is a great example. When we are in a crowded elevator, people we may have never seen before are pushed into our intimate zone. Social convention will not allow us to push them away and there is simply no room for us to open up the space. What do we do? We create emotional space. We either stare at the little moving numbers like they are the most fascinating things in the whole world, or we look at the floor. The one unspoken rule is, you never look strangers in the eye when you are jammed up against them in the elevator. That is just too intimate and risks getting yourself slapped or hit. We tolerate the bodily contact forced upon us by the crowded elevator by focusing our eyes elsewhere and pretending it isn't happening.

Keeping this in mind, the wise shepherd will watch the sheep's eyes as they, the sheep, are talking to each other and to the shepherd. The eyes have been called the "windows of the soul," and in this regard at least, that old adage is correct. Where the eyes are focused will tell how the person is using the physical space in the conversation. If the eyes are intimately focused and the space is intimate, the eyes say the use of space is truthful. If, however, the eyes are focused elsewhere (say, "three feet beyond you"), the eyes show that the intimate use of space is just a game and therefore is not to be trusted.

TIME TELLS

Every leader should be aware that time is our most precious commodity. In the business world, the mantra "time is money" is repeated ad nauseum. Likewise, the Bible has countless references encouraging the reader to realize the importance of time and to make wise use of it. Every one of us has exactly 168 hours per week. No more and, unless we die first, no less. Once it is spent, it can never be retrieved or recycled. Obviously, some of those 168 hours will be spent in the necessities of living such as eating or sleeping. Just as obviously, part of that time must be spent fulfilling our obligations—jobs, required maintenance around the house or apartment, and the like. It is the way that we spend whatever is left over that communicates our real priorities.

As hackneyed as that may seem, it is worth remembering because many context problems arise precisely at this point. We assume that our values "ought" to be the values of the other person. After all, our priorities work for us and seem perfectly reasonable to us. From a listening standpoint, the problem with this approach is that we miss what the other person is trying to tell us about him- or herself. Shepherds who cannot hear what their sheep are saying through their use of time risk becoming increasingly irrelevant to what is actually happening in their congregation or office. A saying that was popular in management courses some years ago was, "There they go, and I must run after them, for I am their leader."

Beyond the way we spend time, the way we talk about time also opens many windows into the context by which we decode meaning. Some of us experience time as *chronos,* chronological time. People who experience time as *chronos* relate events in chronological order. For example, if you ask a *chronos* person what his or her day was like, you will likely get a run down of their daily calendar. A teacher, whether in Sunday school or a presenter at a business conference, who experiences time as *chronos* will present the lesson as chronologically as possible—the time flow will be very obvious. Likewise, a preacher who experiences time as *chronos* will organize sermons that have very clear chronological sequences. Such a preacher may prefer a narrative style of preaching so that every sermon tells a story. The worship services and the meetings will likely follow the announced time line as closely as possible.

Other people experience time as *kairos,* the "right" time or the "fullness of time." You can ask such a person what his or her day was like, and you may get, "Oh, nothing happened." This reply does not mean the person was idle or that the person is being evasive. It simply means that, for the person who experiences time as *kairos*, routine activities are simply the nondescript gray background. Unless things stand out as "significantly" good or bad (as subjectively perceived by the speaker), it is as if they did not happen. Teachers or presenters who experience time as *kairos* will present their lessons in order of significance, with the most significant points likely being placed first so that they can be covered, and the less significant points coming near the end. Similarly, preachers who experience time as *kairos* will tend to present their sermons topically, often with the topics building so that the most important point comes last in hopes of stimulating a response from the congregation. Their worship services and meetings will feel "sloppy" to the person who experiences time as *chronos* because the services may or may not start and end on time. But they will start and end "when the time is right."

Of course, neither of these styles is "best," and probably most every church or office will have some people of both basic orientations. Indeed, these basic orientations actually help determine how "free" or discretionary time is defined and used. The wise shepherd will listen to his or her own experience, to see how he or she experiences time. Then, knowing the shepherd's own context, the shepherd is better able to listen between the lines to the sheep, to listen to what their use of time tells about the way to best work with them.

THINGS TEACH

Comedian George Carlin once defined a house as "a place to put your stuff so you can go out and get more stuff." Certainly, the things we possess do teach something about us. Stanford Research Institute regularly produces the Values and Lifestyle Segments (VALS)—an estimate of the kinds of interests that are typical of people at certain demographic levels.[5] Marketing psychologists use tools like the VALS to design marketing strategies targeted to potential customers so that customers will believe the new product is something they simply "must" have. Whether people choose to buy a Lexus or a Kia, for example, they are teaching something about the way they see themselves.

The way we use the things we have also teaches. For example, many parents complain about their teens' messy rooms. The chaos of the room is simply an acting out of the chaos the teen feels in his or her life. If parents can listen between the lines and hear the mess as a statement of their teen's life, rather than hearing it as an affront to their authority or expectations, they may be able to create a better working relationship with their teen.

The same principle applies in leadership settings, as experienced in both the church and corporate world. Leaders, especially religious leaders, often complain that the sheep leave everything for them to do. "I am supposed to be the leader, so why do I have to set up and take down tables for every meeting?" The actions of the sheep are teaching the shepherd something about their feelings of ownership of the meeting, and perhaps even of the congregation or business itself.

Levels of giving also teach about the person's feelings of ownership. Jesus said, "For where your treasure is, there your heart will be also" (Matt. 6:21). This is perhaps why Jesus became so excited about the widow he observed in the temple (Mark 12:41–43). In terms of raw dollars (to use a modern term), what she gave was very small. What she gave, however, was everything she had. She truly did give more than all the rest. Religious professionals will have to follow their own church's established procedures and their own conscience about knowing who gives how much. They can and should look at the overall picture. Census figures and various commercial companies can give data about the average income for a specific zip code. These figures will allow religious leaders to estimate what the giving "ought" to be and then compare the congregation's average giving with that estimate. If there is a significant difference between the actual and the estimate, the congregation may be teaching the shepherd about how much "heart" they have in the congregation.

Perhaps this is one reason why some people react so negatively to discussions involving money. Whether we're discussing a corporate, government, religious, or even marital context, budget battles are usually the nastiest. For many people, money is the primary means of expressing power. Fights over the budget are really fights over who holds the power—over who "counts" and who does not. Accusations about "always preaching about money" are best heard as teaching about the disconnect between the shepherd's priorities and the flock's. Bringing out sermon logs or meeting minutes to show how seldom money is the topic misses the point. The real issue is who has the power to determine what will actually happen. Shepherds who can listen between the lines nondefensively can learn a lot about where their followers' hearts are, and can then more effectively decide how to respond.

SUMMARY

Listening involves a complex process of decoding meaning. The meaning in the message is in the words the speaker chooses, the context the speaker and listener bring to the relationship, and the actions that each participant brings to the relationship. Each piece of the listening process is necessary to accurately "listen between the lines." The next chapter will give some suggestions for applying these skills to leadership.

Living into the Lesson

1. Begin with a self-analysis. On a scale of one to ten with one being "I need a sledge hammer hitting me before I get the message" and ten being "I easily pick up on intended meanings," how well do you think you do at "reading between the lines?" If married, ask your spouse to rate you as well. Ask three coworkers. Ask three friends. Does the response from others validate your self-analysis?

2. What are some of your personal biases that cause you to communicate/listen the way you do?
3. What are your emotional triggers? How well do you recognize them?
4. What kinds of topics or situations tend to make you more reactive when communicating? What is one step you could take to help you become more responsive and less reactive?
5. The text makes the point that "sin" (our human imperfections) interferes with our ability to listen properly. Do you agree? Why or why not?
6. Who is the person you know whose actions most closely matched his or her words? How was this person different from others you know? Did you respect this person more/less/equally compared to others you know? Why? Why is this congruency important for a leader?
7. Are you aware of the physical space described in the text? How do you react when someone "violates" one of your zones (such as coming too close)?
8. How does your use of time communicate your core values to others? How do you respond when someone demonstrates different feelings towards use of time than you do (maybe *chromos* versus *kairos*)?
9. How do you interpret the way others use "stuff?" How does your own use of "stuff" communicate your values to others?

2

BOSS OR LEADER?

The boss drives people; the leader coaches them.
The boss depends on authority, the leader on good will.
The boss inspires fear; the leader inspires enthusiasm.
The boss says I; the leader says WE. The boss fixes the blame for the breakdown; the leader fixes the breakdown.
The boss says, GO; the leader says, Let's GO!

—H. GORDON SELFRIDGE, AMERICAN-BORN FOUNDER OF BRITISH DEPARTMENT STORE SELFRIDGES

Any person can be a boss, meaning that person has been given positional authority. People must do as you say simply by virtue of the title you hold. If you are a pastor, company manager, CEO, or shift manager at a fast food restaurant, there are folks under you to whom you can give orders and expect those orders to be followed. What every good leader realizes is that just because you are the boss does not mean you are a leader. A leader is one with relational authority—people follow you because of who you are, not necessarily because of your title.[1] We have seen countless situations in companies and churches where the boss was not the leader. This dynamic can create substantial tension between the one with positional authority who expects to be obeyed and the one with the relational authority whom people actually follow.

If you want to be a boss, this is probably not the right book for you. The skill sets required to achieve "boss" status will not be the focus of this book. While we realize this is a very sweeping generality, in most cases if you work hard enough, schmooze the right people, and/or earn enough seniority, chances are you will eventually be given positional authority deserved or not. It takes an entirely different set of skills and much effort, however, to be a leader. You have already learned one key skill for leadership—how to listen to your flock. A boss does not have to listen. The flock is supposed to listen to the boss and do whatever the boss says. In order for you to gain relational authority the flock must first of all feel that you care enough to listen to them.

The second key skill needed to turn a boss into a leader is the ability to "diagnose" your flock. In later chapters we will deal with specific types of sheep within your flock, how to recognize them, and how to most effectively lead them. By now you may be beginning to realize that being a good shepherd is a lot of hard work. Framed in the simplest terms, being a boss is easy—you tell people what to do and they do it. Good shepherds, both ancient and modern, take time for each individual sheep and understand the differences throughout the flock. It is their custom to bring the sheep together each evening in order to check over each sheep one by one looking for injury or disease. If anything unusual is found the sheperd marks that sheep and comes back to it later to tend the need. A good shepherd's job is not finished simply because the sheep have arrived at their pasture for the evening. Knowing your flock will be a time consuming, often thankless, task, but the rewards of increased health and productivity in your flock, as well as your effectiveness as a leader, will be more than worth it.

Let's begin with a basic understanding of how the flock, as a whole, operates and how leaders and bosses operate within the flock.

BELONGING

Have you ever tried to work out your local ecosystem on a flow chart? Living systems tend not to fit well within nice, neat categories. There is so much variance that a good bit of effort is required to understand, and operate within, a living system. A machine, on the other hand, will continue operating exactly the same day after day unless modified or broken. You can always depend on a machine to do exactly what you expect it to do. Your car today will be the same car tomorrow. It won't have learned, grown, or changed in any way without intentional modification or a breakdown. A "boss" likes things in order, unchanging, with clearly defined rules and expectations. A "leader" learns to adapt as the system shifts and actively seeks to help the system grow.

Congregations are living systems and, as such, have the same properties as any other system, from single-celled organisms to multinational corporations. One of the prime characteristics of any system is homeostasis, that is, the tendency to keep on doing the same things. When people in a congregation resist change, they are not necessarily being stubborn or oppositional. They are simply testifying to the power of homeostasis.

Saint Paul, in the New Testament, gives personal testimony to how strong this force is within the spiritual realm. Our paraphrase of Romans 7:14–17 is: "I don't understand myself. As soon as I think I have this following Christ thing all figured out, just as I think I have beaten my old sinful habits, that's the very time I do the dirty, base things that I know I should not do." Families, too, can get stuck in doing things that no longer work. For example, parents can find themselves constantly yelling at their child even though they know they should not yell and know, in fact, the yelling does nothing to win the child's cooperation. Yet they keep on yelling. That is homeostasis at work.

Human relational systems tend to maintain homeostasis through negative feedback loops. This may sound confusing, but the concept is a little easier to understand by looking at a very common, nonhuman example—the thermostat in your house. Let's assume that you have set the thermostat on your central air conditioning unit at eighty. Let's also assume that your thermostat, like many, has a two-degree comfort zone. That means it will keep the house within plus or minus two degrees of the desired temperature. When the temperature in the house reaches eighty-two, the air conditioner comes on and cools the house to seventy-eight, where upon the thermostat is "satisfied" and shuts the air conditioner off. This gives an average temperature of eighty in the house, just as the setting required. What is happening inside the thermostat is that a bimetallic coil is winding or unwinding in response to the temperature change. This, in turn, tips a mercury switch one way or the other to either close a circuit, making the air conditioner turn on, or open a circuit, shutting it off.

What does this have to do with human behavior? Each of us has a certain self-image, formed by our interactions with others. Just as with the thermostat, our self-image has a certain comfort zone. As long as we are within the range of that comfort zone, we feel "like me" and, therefore, comfortable. If, however, we start performing below what we believe we "ought" to do, we start feeling guilty and anxious. This motivates us to increased action so that we get back "to where we belong." Similarly, if we start performing much better than we believe we "ought" to, we unconsciously begin to mess up so that we get back "to where we belong." Either way, the point is that any time we feel "not me," we will take whatever steps are necessary to get back to homeostasis, back to "where we belong."

This is as true of groups as it is of individuals. Take, for example, the pastor who wants to institute a contemporary worship service in a previously very traditional congregation. The pastor may initially gain a favorable response to the proposal from various key members of the congregation. After the service is actually instituted, however, some opposition is almost sure to arise. The more successful the contemporary service, the stronger the opposition. The "reason" for the opposition probably will have a note of truth. The opposition may complain about overcrowding, lack of parking space, the extra noise, or a host of other issues. But the real issue is not any of these presenting problems.

Here, again, listening between the lines is necessary. The real issue is the anxieties generated by change—the feeling that the congregation is "not us" any more. Unless the pastor recognizes what is going on and deals with the underlying anxiety, any efforts at soothing the mounting conflict will likely be doomed to failure. That is because the further from the comfort zone a system moves, the greater the anxiety and therefore the greater the push to get back to "where it belongs." The power of homeostasis is so strong that some churches will even self-destruct as they grow to prevent getting too far from their comfort zone. Chris has served a church that was known for this very attribute. The church would start growing but, eventually, it would self-destruct almost to the point of closing before starting to grow again. The "average" of this cycle produced a small, family church that was the comfort zone for most members. You can apply this same example to any business trying to change by offering a new product, a new marketing scheme, or a new way of doing anything. Some will resist, not because the idea is bad, but because it's "not us."

The difference between a boss and a leader really shines through when wrestling with this concept of homeostasis. If the change is the boss's idea then the boss could not care less whether the flock is comfortable with the idea or not. "We're going to change and that's final!" is the attitude of the boss. We have seen several issues of severe conflict, and even splits, within congregations because the pastor told the congregation exactly what they were going to do whether they liked it or not. A congregation can rebel with their checkbooks (withholding giving) and their feet (leaving). They may also exhibit passive aggressive behavior by not openly bad mouthing the project, but a previously very active person suddenly becomes very inactive within the church. In a corporation the flock will rarely walk out the door, but they may actively start to seek other employment opportunities. Their effectiveness and efficiency decrease. Their loyalty to the company wanes.

Contrast this attitude with that of a leader. A leader understands the principle of homeostasis and uses it to his or her advantage. What causes the thermostat to kick on? The temperature in the room becomes too hot or cold. In other words, the environment becomes uncomfortable. In order to change homeostasis the effective shepherd does the hard work of showing the flock that the current temperature is not the ideal setting. A good leader never goes into a meeting for a vote without knowing the outcome ahead of time. The only way to accomplish that feat is by spending a lot of time with the flock beforehand, gaining their trust and convincing them that the next pasture over is better than the one they are currently in. Once the flock is convinced to move, however, the shepherd must continue to reassure them that the decision they made was the correct one. Assuming that the conflict is ended simply because a decision has been made can be a fatal mistake.

While homeostasis is a powerful force, the comfort zone can be changed in human systems just as it can be changed with an air conditioner. If a homeowner is willing to pay the price, the thermostat will just as happily keep the house at sixty-five degrees as at eighty. The new homeostasis will be maintained as diligently as the old. Change, however, will not happen without deliberate and appropriate effort. On a thermostat, one must intentionally move the temperature selector to change the range within which the bimetal coil will operate. In human systems, too, deliberate effort is necessary. The church we referred to earlier has learned to overcome their old homeostasis and is now a growing, thriving congregation. This did not happen through simply hoping, but through intentional effort.

BOUNDARIES

A second property of all systems is boundaries. In single-celled organisms, the boundary is the cell membrane. Human relational systems are much more complex and usually have two kinds of boundaries. One of these is physical, analogous to the cell membrane. Nations have established, and usually guarded, borders. Churches, like families, own or rent property. Within these physical boundaries, the church can largely determine what happens and when. The church can also take appropriate steps to limit access by outsiders. For example, Chris served a downtown church in a high-traffic area of the city where it was necessary to post signs in the parking lots limiting public, nonchurch, and business parking. Most churches also put locks on their doors and limit who has the keys.

A good leader can often gauge the flock's feelings towards the outside world by observing the manner in which the flock guards their physical boundaries. If a pastor arrives at a church to find that only one person has a key to the building and all requests for access must go through that person, then the pastor can deduce some control issues might be at play within the congregation. On the other hand, if a pastor arrives at his or her new charge to find that everyone at the church has his or her own key, coming and going as they please, the pastor might be concerned about the boundary issues within the congregation. A church with very strict rules about what outside groups can and cannot use the church, or how they can use the church, might signal the shepherd that the flock mistrusts the community around them. The potential examples are endless. The point is that physical boundaries, while not revealing everything, can provide the observant shepherd with some initial data as to the flock's behavior.

The other kind of boundary in human systems is relational. Every human system has a way of defining and enforcing who belongs. Indeed, psychiatrist Alfred Adler believed that belonging is one of two absolutely essential human psychological needs. In his mind, belonging is as optional to psychological health as breathing is to physical health. The other need, equally essential, is the need to constantly improve one's self.

Our criminal justice system provides striking evidence for just how potent the need to belong is. Solitary confinement is the most severe punishment that can be imposed short of death. Some of us, the so-called extroverts, need to belong to many others, while others of us, the so-called introverts, need to belong to only a few select others, but all of us need to belong. Without feeling connected, we feel as though we are next to death.

All organizations—companies, fraternities/sororities, faith communities—have some sort of initiation ritual to define who belongs. In Jewish synagogues, that is a bar or bas mitzvah. In Christian churches, it is baptism. Other religious bodies have their own rituals. Whatever the ritual in question may be, all of them define and enforce belonging. This powerful sense of belonging is why church splits, when they happen, are so traumatic. The closest analog is marriage. When a man and woman marry, they are united as one (Gen. 2:24). Having officiated at literally hundreds of weddings in our years of pastoral ministry, we have yet to meet a couple who did not believe "till death do us part" would be their destiny, even those who had been previously married. For that reason, when a divorce happens, it feels like losing an arm or a leg, even under the best of circumstances. As the 1989 black comedy "War of the Roses" strikingly illustrates, it can go downhill from there. When churches split, or even when an individual leaves, it is a divorce—a declaration that we formerly belonged together, but no longer. I do not belong to you and you do not belong to me. That is always very painful, as anyone who has lived through the experience can testify. Tragically, like a divorce, the hurt and anger can linger for years following the final break.

In this situation the difference between boss and leader becomes glaring. A boss coming into a new situation where there has been a split of some kind will seek to impose his or her own agenda without consideration for what has previously happened. This can be even truer when the new boss was part of the previous "pre-split" system. The desire to "move on" is so strong that all reference to the past is squashed or ridiculed.

The wise shepherd who serves a congregation that has been through a split in the recent past will actively work to help the sheep heal from their trauma before seeking to implement any new agenda. Divorce and remarriage rarely solves anything beyond changing the players involved in the tragedy (witness the fact that second and third marriages tend to have a higher rate of divorce than first marriages, according to the Census Bureau and Center for Disease Control reports). Similarly, church splits seldom solve the underlying issues. Churches will often calm down briefly after a split, but eventually the same issues will arise even if under different presenting symptoms.

Once again, listening between the lines to hear the pain underneath the glib responses will give the shepherd openings to help the flock finally heal. Based on our experience, this is all the more important because, like divorce, a church split often affects the members' relationship with God. The spiritual and human belonging needs are inseparably tied, and therefore what hurts one will also hurt the other. Conversely, what helps one will help the other. The Bible reminds us that people cannot claim to love a God they have never visibly seen if they cannot love other human beings around them who they can see and touch (1 John 4:20). Later chapters in this book will suggest some specific ways shepherds can help the various kinds of sheep deal with their relational boundaries.

Systems express these belonging needs in two fundamental ways. Healthy systems are open. A good analogy of an open system is a human cell. The cell membrane contains the cell and protects the cell. Yet the membrane also allows nutrients to come into the cell, either passively (such as by diffusion) or through active transport. The membrane also allows for the flow out of the cell to the cell's environment. This is not just a matter of getting rid of waste products. A human neuron, for example, fires because of the flow of sodium and potassium ions into and out of the cell. The two-way flow is absolutely essential for cellular health.

Healthy human systems, too, allow for the free flow in and out of the system. Churches influence their surrounding culture, and are, in turn, influenced by their surrounding culture. Individual members come into the church to become reconnected with God and their core values, and then go back to their everyday lives to embody those connections. In doing so, they influence the culture, even when their religious faith is not explicitly mentioned. Take, for example, a woman who is employed by a large corporation and who also has an active religious faith. Her faith tells her that she should care for others, so when she hears that a coworker has had a personal tragedy or loss, she may organize others in the work center to send a card or flowers or other appropriate expressions of caring. These religious acts of caring, though never explicitly identified as religious, positively impact the morale of the workplace, making the workers, and thus the company, more efficient. Conversely, this same woman will bring her experiences in the workplace to her church. She will see the business of running the church in terms that she learned in the workplace and will expect the church to do its business (however the church would define that) at least as efficiently as the company does its business.

On a broader level, most evangelical Christian churches believe that part of their God-given mission is to reach out to non-Christians and bring them into relationship with Christ. Through their evangelistic efforts, they seek to transform culture and infuse a strong sense of morality throughout it. Yet the strategies for evangelism that actually work will inevitably be shaped by the way businesses do their marketing. This is constantly changing, as businesses devise better ways to create a "need" for their products. If a church is to effectively sell its "product" (that is, a relationship with Christ), it will have to adopt the same kinds of strategies as the businesses use. Perhaps an illustration will be helpful here. The generation that won World War II placed a great deal of value on the ideals of being responsible and socially conscious. Churches could draw them by selling the idea that joining the church was a great way to make society a better place.

The baby boomer generation was sold on the importance of direct experience. The 1960s rock guitarist Jimi Hendrix sang that he was the one who had to live with the consequences of his actions so the world should let him live however he chose.[2] This attitude reflected the attitude of many baby boomers. Churches could draw boomers by promising them a great religious experience, free from all the perceived boring ritualism of their parents. To the boomers, the rituals of the church were a way for those in authority to tell them how they "ought" to experience God, and they wanted to find their own form of expression.

Children of boomers, the Gen-Xers, lived through "the pill," the advent of dual-career homes, latch-key kids, and the explosion of divorces in the 1960s, so they both want relationships and yet are highly suspicious of them. To win Gen-Xers, churches must show that they contribute to solid, satisfying relationships. The children of the Gen-Xers are now coming into their own. While it is too early to yet tell how they will define themselves, one early piece of evidence is that the new generation seems to be rebelling against the Gen-X idea of relativism. A hallmark of postmodernity, which really found its voice in the Gen-Xers, is that whatever works for you is just as valuable as what works for me. Don't try to tell me what to believe and I won't tell you what to believe. The relativistic idea that absolute Truth does not exist, so common among the Gen-X crowd, has created a desire for Truth among the younger generations. Our guess is that in order to capture the upcoming generation the church may very well need to return to its more historic roots and traditions. As evangelical Christians, we believe the message has never changed since Jesus first spoke it. Yet the concept of open system demands that the way the message is presented must change, both influencing and being influenced by the current culture.

The "what happens if it does not" question brings us to the other major way that systems express their belonging needs—closed systems. A closed system either allows for no flow at all—it is static, unchanging—or allows for only one-way flow. The Dead Sea is a good example of this last variation. Closed systems are always unhealthy because they lack the give and take necessary for the health of the system. Cults demonstrate a closed system in a religious context. Almost by definition, cults take members in, but almost immediately the cult will take steps to cut the member off from interaction with the members' families as well as society at large. This is one way the cult leader can maintain control over followers and convince them to accept as perfectly correct beliefs that appear to outsiders as "crazy."

Cult leaders tend to come from one particular kind of sheep that we will describe later. The members of the cults, however, can come from all the types of sheep. It's not that the cult members are crazy. The system is. That is what makes them do seemingly crazy things. The same dynamic works in street gangs. The History Channel began a series in 2007 called *Gangland* profiling major gangs across the United States. Almost every one of the gang members interviewed (many with their face and voice obscured due to fear of retribution) made the comment that the only way to get out of the gang was death. The leaders control the "foot soldiers" by keeping the gang completely closed off from any outsiders.

The Branch Davidians are a perfect example of the closed-system. David Koresh, the charismatic leader of that cult, took many traditional Christian beliefs and spun them in a way that was very different from traditional Christian theology, yet close enough to sound plausible. His ideas and charisma attracted people who were looking for certainty in a very uncertain world. After people joined the Branch Davidians all they were allowed to hear was Koresh's rhetoric, which made them believe that a final war between Good and Evil was imminent, and that the United States government was on the side of Evil. Since that was all they were hearing, it was perfectly logical for them to heavily arm themselves and to fight off the federal agents literally to the last person.

Abusive families form another example of a closed system. The abuser will take steps to isolate the target from others, even other family members. This gives the abuser power over the abused that outsiders cannot understand. Typically a man who is physically or emotionally abusing his wife keeps her stuck by telling her she is "stupid" or "crazy" or "ugly" and that she ought to be grateful she has him because no one else will have her. He will also recruit, either actively or by example, other family members to reinforce his "it's all your fault" message. Because he makes sure she does not have other meaningful relationships, she has nothing to contradict these messages. For her, they are reality, and thus women who truly are gifted and competent act as though they deserve the abuse.

The "boss" model also prefers to work in a closed system, though on a significantly less severe scale than the previous examples. A boss is not interested in feedback. He or she is looking for the flock to fall in line as they are told. The primary issue is always the vision of the boss. Those who argue with the boss, or oppose the boss's vision in any way, are usually ostracized. This can potentially occur in several ways, such as lack of advancement or by being left out of the decision-making process. In severe cases we have seen persons in churches and businesses ignored or avoided by those not wishing to upset the boss.

A leader thrives in the open-system model. Rather than seeing feedback and interaction as a threat, a good leader views both as ways to make a good thing better. The wise shepherd actively encourages appropriate interaction from the flock while maintaining overall leadership of the "big picture." A shepherd is even willing to step aside in certain cases and let one of the flock take the lead. Boundaries are well defined, but not inflexible. In subsequent chapters, we will look at how various kinds of sheep set their boundaries and what the direction of health might be.

RULES

The final characteristic of all systems is rules. Every system has a structure that keeps it operating predictably. Newtonian physics used to talk about "laws" by which our physical world invariably operates. Now we know, through quantum physics, that there is a lot more variability in our physical world than we formerly believed. Still, while our world does not operate by invariable "laws," it does operate predictably enough through rules. We can be fairly confident that if we drop a book, it will fall down to the floor, not up to the ceiling.

Our human relational systems allow for many variations. Our rules vary by gender, culture, ethnicity, and socioeconomic status, just to name some of the major variables. For example, many young boys growing up in a working-class neighborhood have been taught the rule "Big boys don't cry." There were many times you might feel like crying, but the tears simply will not come. You have to follow the "rule" or risk being ostracized by the other boys. Even though we now know better, it is still hard for many adult men raised with this rule to allow tears to come, and so they pass the same rule along to their sons. Rules are that powerful in shaping our behavior.

Sometimes our rules are overt. The theater is an excellent metaphor for these rules. In a theater, all of the action that the audience sees takes place on what the actors call front stage. Our front stage rules are rules that we are explicitly taught. If they are not verbally stated, they are explicitly defined by behavior. The "big boys don't cry" rule of childhood was one such front stage rule. Another example is the rule that it is wrong for a preacher to have sex with a member of the congregation (other than his or her spouse, of course). Sadly, it still happens, and it always damages the preacher, the one with whom the relationship occurred, and the entire congregation after the illicit relationship is revealed. This brings up an important point about our front stage rules. Knowing them does not always imply following them. Look at the way many motorists treat posted speed limits, for example.

Front stage rules include the rules of dress for congregation members. Even congregations that accept jeans and casual dress for the worshipers would likely find the same dress unacceptable for the preacher in the pulpit. The same women who might wear short shorts to the mall might never wear those shorts to church. The point here is not whether these rules are right or wrong. The point is that even if no one ever explicitly says, "This is our church's dress code," everyone knows it because it is modeled so consistently.

Even with all their variations, front stage rules seldom cause us trouble. They are explicitly stated or understood. We know what the expectations are, so we can easily make a conscious decision to follow them or not to follow them. We usually know what the consequences are for not following them, so we make a free choice.

Back stage rules are a completely different animal. In theater jargon, "back stage" is the area behind the curtain, which the audience never sees. There are even things back stage that the actors are not aware of. Still, the activity back stage makes possible all that is seen on front stage. Our back stage rules govern our behavior perhaps more powerfully than our front stage rules because, by definition, they are covert, and therefore they are not open to examination and conscious decision.

Bob and Sue, in chapter 1, were living out some of their back stage rules. Bob's rule was, "My spouse has to take care of the parts of me that I don't want to deal with." No one ever actually told him this rule. If they had, it would be front stage. No, Bob learned this rule by watching the way his mother took care of his father. That was, for him, the way it was "supposed" to be. Sue's parents, however, had a more equalitarian relationship. They openly talked about most items, so Sue and her siblings learned how to solve problems by open communication. They never taught her that was the way marriage "ought" to be. It just became one of Sue's back stage rules.

Wherever they come from, our back stage rules comprise our "Personal Ten Commandments." In choosing that metaphor, we do not mean to imply that there will be ten, or any other certain number. We do mean that we will act as though these were handed down from on high. They are as much a part of us as our heartbeat, and therefore they "ought" to be obvious to anyone. Anyone who does not follow them is clearly wrong.

As Bob and Sue illustrate, because these "Personal Ten Commandments" come from the personal background of and are hidden even from the person following them, we usually become aware of these "Personal Ten Commandments" by transgressing them, which is something akin to stepping on a landmine. Sue could not have known she was stepping on a landmine with Bob because they had never talked about the issue before, and besides, her rule is that you always talk about problems and solve them jointly.

Anyone who has ever been a first-time visitor in a church, whether established or new, may have also run across someone's

"Personal Ten Commandments." Have you ever found that you were sitting in someone's pew? If so, perhaps you thought to yourself, "I didn't see a 'reserved' sign. I didn't see their name on this pew. How was I to know?" You may have even thought, "What's the big deal? There are plenty of other places to sit. Why do I have to move?" Still, most of us in that situation would move because a very common front stage rule is "You are supposed to be 'nice' in church."

Admiral Hyman Rickover, the father of the nuclear navy, said, "It is necessary for us to learn from other people's mistakes. You will not live long enough to make them all yourself." The wise shepherd will apply Admiral Rickover's principle in listening between the lines to the congregation. The shepherd does not have to personally step on all the landmines in a congregation to learn where they are. A shepherd who tries to find all of the landmines personally will end up too injured to lead. Bosses, on the other hand, do not care about the landmines. They set them off with little concern for the consequences. Listen to the stories the sheep tell. The stories we tell about ourselves, as individuals and as collectives, give very strong clues to our back stage rules.

Allow us a personal example. When Wayne was growing up, his father often said, "Son, the world will often kick you down. But as long as you can get back up one more time than they kick you down, you are still a man." Not only did Wayne learn some rules about manhood from this oft-repeated statement, he also learned our family's dominant story. We are Survivors. Life is hard and bad things happen, but we are Survivors. He often told stories about himself and his other family members that reinforced this story.

Congregations, too, have a dominant story that gives clues to their back stage rules. Across denominational lines, for example, the county-seat "First Church" often has a story line that says, "We are the society church. We always have been. People who come here are the social and economic upper crust of our community." The pastor of such a congregation who ignores this story and invites homeless people into the congregation would be stepping on a major landmine. The pastor might well be able to get this same congregation to give generously to the local homeless shelter, but to invite "those" people into the congregation would violate one of the congregation's Personal Ten Commandments. The congregation members may never overtly express their dissatisfaction with such a move. More than likely, they would talk only among themselves and ignore the homeless people who did come to worship, pointedly communicating nonverbally, "You do not belong here." In this way they can follow the front stage rule about being "nice" and their back stage rule about who belongs. The opposition will likely come to the pastor in other, much more indirect, areas, and unless the pastor in this situation starts listening between the lines, he or she may never realize why a previously good ministry suddenly, and seemingly inexplicably, went downhill. The reality is that pastor stepped on a landmine and his or her ministry was damaged in the resulting "explosion."

While the specific back stage rules will vary among congregations, just as they do among individuals, no individual or congregation is exempt. Take, for example, the small, rural congregation that professes a front stage belief in the importance of evangelism. They even hold week-long evangelistic services twice a year. Yet, as the pastor listens to this congregation, the stories they tell are of how everyone in the congregation is related. This story uncovers the back stage rule, "You must be a relative to belong here." Of course they have not had a new member join in years, except for other relatives. The congregation members are not being hypocritical about their professed belief in evangelism. They are just illustrating that, because they are covert, back stage rules often trump front stage rules.

In his explanation of human behavior, Adler called these Personal Ten Commandments the person's "Style of Life." Some people have the style of the "Big Man on Campus," that is, they might be following the story that they must be dominant in their social groups. Certainly someone following the "boss" model would fit this idea, but many of the flock carry this picture of themselves. A person also might be a "Getter," that is, they might be setting themselves up so that they "get" from others either by manipulation or being "helpless." Listening between the lines will usually reveal the previously hidden Personal Ten Commandments. Each of the types of sheep discussed in subsequent chapters will tend to have a unique Style of Life. By recognizing the sheep's Personal Ten Commandments, the shepherd is in a better position to bring these rules out to the front stage where they can be examined and, if necessary, possibly changed.

A big difference between a boss and a leader is how back stage and front stage rules are treated. With a boss the only back stage rule is "You do what I say." Most others are ignored. On the front stage a boss might profess to want to value the opinions of others, but what happens when someone presents an idea contrary to the boss? He or she might speak of the importance of family time, but what happens if the rest of the flock does not work as many hours or give as much as the boss? We have seen many bosses operate exclusively on the back stage. They are never openly critical or confrontational, but when someone steps on a landmine that person will be noticeably cut off.

A leader seeks to understand the back stage rules in order to successfully operate on the front stage. George Barna, who makes his living looking at church trends and demographics, noted in 1998 that the average pastoral tenure was four years in Protestant churches.[3] The same study showed that the most effective ministry for a pastor takes place between years five and fourteen. We heartily agree with Mr. Barna's findings and feel with today's confusing and constantly changing society this rule has only become truer in the years since this study. It takes years of concentrated effort to discover and change a back stage rule. Some of these rules are worth the effort, but often they aren't. Rather than spending the effort to change these rules, the wise shepherd will discover these rules and make use of them. A shepherd does not necessarily go out of his or her way to avoid confronting an issue that must be confronted, but if the shepherd realizes up front what he or she is dealing with then it becomes much easier to choose the best course of action. A shepherd is not seeking to impose his or her will upon the flock as a boss is, but rather to guide them to places of safety and health.

SUMMARY

Being a leader is not easy. Jesus states that the road to salvation is a bumpy, narrow dirt road, while the road to destruction is an eight-lane freeway (Matt. 7:13–14). The same can be said of leaders and bosses. Being a boss is relatively easy. You tell everyone what to do and they do it. Rarely, though, does this path lead to personal satisfaction or professional satisfaction from the followers, even when monetary success is achieved. Being a leader can be very lonely and tedious. The effort required to shepherd a flock is tremendous. In the end, however, the effort pays off in the form of a healthy, happy flock who grow to their full potential, often surpassing a shepherd's wildest expectations. A farmer cannot enjoy the harvest without first doing the backbreaking work of tilling and planting. The "boss" model wants to reap without sowing (Matt. 25:26).

The effort the leader must put in requires an understanding of the flock system as a whole, as well as understanding the nuances of the different sheep. This chapter has given a basic overview as to how to understand the flock as a system. The next few chapters will seek to help the wise shepherd respond appropriately to the various types of sheep.

Living into the Lesson

1. In your place of leadership do you think you currently hold positional authority, relational authority, or both?

2. Who are some of the people in your flock with relational authority?
3. Who can you identify within your flock who may have positional authority but not relational authority? What steps do you need to take to improve their leadership?
4. Identify the "comfort zone" of your flock. What is their ideal situation? What have you seen happen to push them out of this comfort zone that caused their negative feedback loop to kick in? What specific steps do you need to take to change the homeostasis within your flock?
5. What types of changes make you personally feel anxious? What steps do you take to overcome your anxiety?
6. Is your flock an open or closed boundary system? What clues led you to this deduction? Do you feel your flock needs to be more or less open?
7. What intentional steps do you take within your flock to help the members feel like they "belong?"
8. How has culture influenced how your flock conducts business and how has your flock influenced the culture around it?
9. What "front stage" rules exist within your flock? What "back stage" rules have you discovered? How do these rules impact your leadership? Ask a close friend or coworker to help you discover your personal "back stage" rules that may impact how you lead.

3

WEDNESDAY SHEEP

Nobody realizes that some people expend tremendous energy merely to be normal.

—ALBERT CAMUS, FRENCH NOBEL PRIZE WINNING NOVELIST AND PLAYWRIGHT

We begin examining our flock by listening to Wednesday Sheep. These are the sheep we all think we are—the so-called "normal" sheep. The odds are, most of you reading this book, and most of your flock, probably are Wednesday Sheep, because by definition "normal" is really a statistical concept that means "like most others." It does not necessarily imply "healthy" or "desirable." In a perfect statistical distribution, about 66 percent of people will be in the "normal" or average range. While there is no research available to verify that the kinds of sheep truly are distributed as predicted by statistics, it seems reasonable to believe that most sheep fall somewhere in the "normal" range. Based on that assumption, about 66 percent of sheep in any flock—be it church, business, or any other organization—and 66 percent of shepherds/leaders within those organizations, will be Wednesday Sheep. With that assumption out in the open, we will look at what really is "normal" so that the shepherd can determine who the Wednesday Sheep are and how best to help them grow.

Do you recall from the introduction the three primary functions of a shepherd? Feed, protect, lead. In other words, your job as a shepherd is to help each sheep in your flock grow to full health and potential. Sheep, however, are not all alike. Different types of sheep require different food, different amounts of protection, and different methods of leadership. These next few chapters, beginning with this one, will assist you indentifying the types of sheep in your flock and then how to properly care for them.

CHARACTERISTICS OF THE WEDNESDAY SHEEP

Wednesday Sheep have a healthy respect for rules. They are clear about their rules, and they can enforce these rules when appropriate. Yet they are also able to renegotiate these rules when necessary. Tim and Carole are a good case in point. When they were young parents, they decided that it was important to who they were as a family that the whole family eat at least one meal together every day. When the kids were preschool age and even in elementary school, Tim and Carole were able to enforce this rule, even though it was not always convenient. They felt good about this and believed it was responsible for the feelings of closeness all members of their family experienced. When the kids moved to the teen years, however, it became obvious that this rule was becoming unworkable. They called a family meeting and discussed how they could adapt to their new situation and still maintain the closeness all members of the family agreed they wanted. They decided that they were going to move to eating one meal per week as a family, and at the same time they were going to check in with each other every day by some means, whether face to face or through voice mail, e-mail, or whatever worked. This became the new rule, and it worked well for them. It was not always easy, but they all understood the benefits, so they did what was necessary to make it work.

The same characteristic applies to institutions that are truly healthy. One example might be the church Wayne attended during seminary. This church was in Georgetown, a very exclusive area of Washington, D.C. At one time, its members were the financially elite of the D.C. area. Over time, however, the character of Georgetown changed. While the wealthy were still very much in evidence, many avant-garde young adults also flocked to the area. The church was faced with a decision: do we, the church, continue to enforce our dress code, or do we open our doors to anyone and everyone regardless of dress? After much open deliberation, the church decided to change its rule. As a result, it was not at all uncommon to see a man wearing a $500 business suit sitting next to a man wearing ragged blue jeans and a t-shirt. The change in rules allowed the church to continue to grow and prosper despite the change in its community.

Wednesday Sheep are similarly able to negotiate changes in roles when necessary. An example of someone who was not able to effectively change roles was masterfully portrayed by Robert Duvall in the 1979 film *The Great Santini*. Santini was a successful Marine Corps officer who tried to run his family the way he ran his unit. As a good officer, he knew what was best for those he loved. He wanted desparately to shape his son into the kind of man who would follow in his footsteps. But his son (portrayed by Michael O'Keefe, who received a Best Supporting Actor Academy Award nomination for this role), had other ideas about his life. He loved his father, but he was not his father. One of the climactic moments of the film showed a basketball game between father and son. O'Keefe for the first time in his life began to beat his father at the game. The rule was, "No one beats the commander at anything," so

Santini tried to verbally bully his son into giving in. The son tasted victory and pressed his attack. Finally, Santini could not take it any more, and bounced the basketball off his son's head several times. The game, which started as a great bonding time between father and son, ended in bitterness. Though he truly loved his son, indeed he loved his whole family, he could not stand to lose. He could not give up his role as the one who is *always* in charge.

"Santini" illustrates one point about Wednesday Sheep that should not be missed. Not every Wednesday Sheep falls in the "ideal" range. Santini was a loving family man and a successful Marine Corps pilot, yet he was also heading toward alcoholism due to his inability to face some parts of himself. Additionally, his inability to renegotiate roles created even more unnecessary pain in his life. A primary function of a shepherd in leading Wednesday Sheep is to help them understand the rules and responsibilities they have at their current position, but also help them redefine their role when the situation changes. Failing to help a Wednesday Sheep negotiate change can lead to ineffectiveness and inefficiency in a corporation, and a lot of pain in personal or church situations.

Ed and Charlotte are an example of a couple who were better able to renegotiate roles when necessary. Both were good parents. At the same time, both were very hard-driving and, consequently, very successful in their own careers. They had somehow managed to negotiate a balance between home life and career that worked for them. That is, it worked until Ed had a heart attack. This threw the whole family for a loop. Ed was not a smoker, he worked out at the gym regularly, he and Charlotte ate a healthy diet, yet he had a very serious heart attack. He survived, thanks to the rapid response of paramedics and neighbors who knew CPR, yet his recovery was slow. During his recovery, the family reorganized to do what was necessary for Ed. Charlotte and the kids dropped out of most of their many social involvements to make sure someone from the family was always present with Ed. Gradually, as Ed began to be able to take back more of his self-care, the family members shifted back to their previous activities. Six months after Ed's heart attack, the cardiologist gave him the "all clear" and the family was in most ways functioning as they had before the heart attack changed their lives.

Ed and Charlotte illustrate that Wednesday Sheep, when they are functioning well, can change and adapt to almost any circumstance of life. They can face life on its own terms. Wednesday Sheep who are not functioning quite as well may have more problems changing with circumstances. Still, by definition, Wednesday Sheep can make changes to their rules and roles as necessary to make sure that at least most of their needs are getting met.

Wednesday Sheep exemplify appropriate boundaries. To use the language popularized by Transactional Analysis, they live an "I'm okay, you're okay" style of belonging.[1] In their families, work, and churches, they ensure that their needs are met and at the same time they accept others' differences. While none of us perfectly lives out this principle—this is the world after the fall, after all—Wednesday Sheep come closer than any other types of sheep. Another way of saying the same thing is that Wednesday Sheep respect themselves and equally respect others. Ironically, Santini's dominant style in his family was likely born out of respect for his family members. He "knew" they were okay and therefore they could be better than they were. The irony is that his actions did not have the good result he intended because he was so fixed in his role that he could not really listen to his family members.

A Wednesday Sheep who came a little closer to the ideal was John. He firmly believed that the King James Version was the only acceptable translation of the Bible. He refused to look at, much less read, any other translation. Yet he actively participated in a Sunday school class where other class members, including the class teachers, regularly read from other translations. He did not insist the others bend to meet his standards, but he also refused to bend his standards to conform to others.

Paul's advice to Timothy fits Wednesday Sheep. Paul suggests that church leaders should be able to manage their own families with mutual respect (1 Tim. 3:4–5). Truly, one's own family can be the most challenging place to live out mutual respect. As Jesus said in a somewhat different context, "Prophets are not without honor except in their own country and in their own house" (Matt. 13:57). Those who love us most know best how to "push our buttons." What differentiates Wednesday Sheep from other sheep is that they do not deliberately set out to push others' buttons, and when they do feel anger or hurt, they take steps to resolve whatever the issues might have been.

Tim and Carole's family life, while emotionally close, was certainly not perfect. Ron, their oldest son, seemed to need to push the limits from the time he was old enough to walk. The first time he was allowed to take the family car on a date, for example, he came home thirty minutes past the established deadline. When he came in the door, Tim and Carole were waiting. They calmly asked for the keys and announced it was too late to talk, but they would talk in the morning. That kept the situation from becoming excessively reactive and gave Ron a night to think about his choices. True to their word, the three of them met in the morning and they jointly decided what Ron would have to do to show that he was ready to handle the responsibility of taking the car out alone again. When Ron lived up to his end of the agreement, Tim and Carole lived up to theirs. Nothing more was said about the incident and Ron did come home on time from that point forward.

The interaction of this family illustrates several characteristics of healthy Wednesday Sheep. While they know that most people do not intend to deliberately hurt others, they recognize that we "all have sinned and fall short of the glory of God" (Rom. 3:23) and therefore things will happen. They do not interpret transgressions of family rules as a personal attack. At the same time, they respect themselves too much to allow transgressions that do occur to go unacknowledged. In Tim and Carole's case, they knew from past experience with Ron that if they had confronted him at the moment, he would have become angry and started yelling, something Carole could not stand. That kind of confrontation violated a strongly held rule she had about children not being disrespectful. She also knew from past experience that if she responded to Ron's yelling the situation would quickly degenerate into name calling and hurt feelings all around. Since they recognized the potential danger, they took steps to allow a cool-down period before the confrontation. Both Tim and Carole respected themselves too much, and Ron too much, to simply ignore his breaking the rules by excusing it as "boys will be boys" or something similar. They also respected each other and Ron too much to simply yell at him or ground him. If they had, he could ignore the lesson as something that had been done "to" him. That would give him no opportunity to learn from the experience. By allowing Ron to be part of the discussion to establish the consequences to help him learn from the incident, they demonstrated respect for him. They demonstrated mutual respect by keeping the focus on behavior, which can be changed, rather than on characteristics like personality, which are exceptionally resistant to change.

Tim and Carole's example is not for families alone. Many times similar situations arise within a company or church. One of your flock may violate the rules or push the limits too far. You have to respect yourself, and the rest of the organization, enough to respond to the rule breaker, but doing so through direct confrontation, even if you have the positional authority to do so, results in nothing but anger and resentment. Tim and Carole, as parents, certainly had positional authority. They could have responded to Ron with any authoritarian method they wished. Instead, they used relational authority, the respect given by Ron, to use the incident to help Ron grow rather than simply punishing him. A shepherd always seeks to help the sheep grow to health, not to punish. As shown in this case, helping the sheep grow to health does not mean allowing transgressions to go unchallenged. Far from it. Rather, the shepherd must wisely decide how to confront the problematic behavior while not alienating the transgressor.

Because Wednesday Sheep operate from a basic, "I'm okay, you're okay" life story, they are able to maintain their belonging even in the midst of disagreements. The Beulah Church's experience demonstrates this trait. On the surface, their conflict was very simple. There were two main families in the congregation. One family wanted its family members to be elected to leadership positions, and the other family wanted its family members to be elected to those same leadership positions. Efforts to work out a compromise proved fruitless. The pastor, recognizing that the presenting issue is not always the real issue, but rather a symptom, decided to deal with the core issue. He had the leaders of both families meet at the altar of the church and had each person pray for his "enemy." Shortly after that, the church was able to elect a slate of leaders that everyone could agree on. While all of the issues between these two families were not solved by that one intervention, the congregation had found a way, with the pastor's leadership, to maintain their belonging without either leaving or creating an internal division that would continue to fester.

LEADING THE WEDNESDAY SHEEP

As the Beulah Church's case shows, Wednesday Sheep, even the most healthy, will require leadership from time to time. What marks Wednesday Sheep is that accurate listening can lead to effective change. If the leader will truly take time to listen to the Wednesday Sheep and respond accordingly, then the Wednesday Sheep will gladly follow their shepherd. Other types of sheep are not always so responsive.

Most of the leader's work with Wednesday Sheep will be in a supportive role. In a church setting, depending on the congregation's expectations, that may involve routine visits to the home from time to time. In an office setting, it means occasionally sitting down in someone's office for an informal chat. It will likely involve talking to people in various informal gatherings and relationship building during meetings. Because Wednesday Sheep are largely able to take care of their own needs, these brief interactions will be enough for them. Yet, although these interactions are usually brief, they still provide vital opportunities for the shepherd to really listen to his or her sheep.

The wise shepherd will listen carefully to the stories the Wednesday Sheep tell during these social occasions. While not one of these stories is likely significant in and of itself—these are social occasions after all, and our usual social rules say we only share "acceptable" stories in such situations—by listening to the patterns of stories, the shepherd can gain insight into the relational health and resources of the sheep.

There are two basic situations in which Wednesday Sheep are likely to need focused leadership, beyond the routine of worship services, social events, and meetings. One of these will be transition times. As pastors, we often joke that we know we'll see people at least during three points in their life—when they "hatch, match, and dispatch," that is, when they are born, when they marry, and when they die. Regardless of our church tradition, these transitional times are tremendous openings for leadership to all our sheep, Wednesday Sheep no less than anyone else.

Other transition times may or may not be as formalized in the church's ritual, but they still provide openings for leadership. When people move, their lives are disrupted and they are particularly open to having their belonging needs met. A custom like a "welcome wagon" can help meet these needs. If you truly want to instill loyalty to your organization in a new employee or church member, the way you treat them when they first move to your area will have a greater impact than at any other point. The move from childhood to adulthood is always momentous, and usually rocky, so rituals to recognize that transition such as confirmation or bar/bas mitzvah can help parents begin the process of reordering their family rules to allow for this new stage of development. Regardless of our theological feelings about divorce, it is a reality and it, too, provides an opportunity for the pastor/shepherd to provide ministry that might otherwise not be there. One often neglected transition (in our opinion) is obtaining one's driver's license for the first time. Having access to the car keys marks a significant increase both in independence and in responsibility. This deserves to be celebrated. Other transitions are not so happy. High among these are the anniversaries of the death of loved ones. A simple phone call or short visit during any of these transition times can yield rich opportunities for ministry, despite their seeming routine nature. Here the shepherd simply has to listen to the stories the sheep tell, celebrating the uplifting parts and, perhaps, crying with the sheep over the hurtful parts.

The other major time Wednesday Sheep likely will need focused leadership is during crisis times, such as Ed's heart attack mentioned earlier. A job loss, whether being fired or simply laid off through corporate "downsizing," is also a crisis for those experiencing it, as anyone who has lived through that can testify. Shepherds who listen carefully can gain helpful clues on to how best to lead in this particular situation. For example, Sally was a blue-collar worker who had been employed in a factory for more than twenty years. When the management decided to close the factory and move its manufacturing overseas, Sally was devastated. As she told her pastor, "I never really loved my job. But I worked hard and every Friday when I got my check, I knew I had earned my pay. Now, for the first time in my life, someone will be paying me for work I didn't do." The shepherd who listens carefully can hear Sally's personal theme, "I must be responsible for myself to be worthwhile." It was that loss of self-worth, as evidenced by her dependence on unemployment insurance, more than the very real financial difficulties, that most disturbed Sally. By accurately diagnosing her theme, the pastor was able to help Sally find new ways of building the self-worth she needed to heal from her unexpected job loss.

Crisis leadership during a major natural or man-made disaster can be especially taxing not only because of the number of people negatively impacted, but also because you, as the shepherd, may have been personally affected. On March 27, 1994, the Goshen United Methodist Church in Piedmont, Alabama, was heavily damaged by a F4 tornado right in the middle of Palm Sunday services. The pastor's daughter was one of twenty people killed in that storm. The pastor had to care for her own injuries, tend her own grief, and also deal with her feelings of responsibility for caring for the injured and grieving members of her flock—a truly overwhelming task for anyone, no matter how emotionally healthy or spiritually connected. These are the kinds of crises that the shepherd should most definitely never try to face alone. There is a line from Mel Brooks' classic comedy *Blazing Saddles* that is very appropriate here. Sheriff Bart looked in a cell to see the "drunk in Number 2" hanging upside down from the top bunk and struggling to right himself. Sheriff Bart asked, "Do you need some help?" The inmate replied, "Oh, all I can get." In mass disaster situations, leaders need all the help they can get.

Fortunately, such situations are exceptionally rare, and many shepherds may go through their entire professional lives without ever confronting a crisis of this magnitude. A more routine, but no less important, issue is selecting Wednesday Sheep to be leaders of the flock. During the week-in and week-out contacts the shepherd has with the sheep, some basic themes are bound to emerge. The shepherd will want to listen for sheep who are secure enough to admit the kinds of "normal" flaws that are just part of the human condition. At the same time, these admissions should be socially appropriate (as defined by the general culture in which the church is located). Any time the shepherd hears something and thinks, "Ouch, I'm glad that's not me they are talking about," that is a big caution flag. Similarly, the absence of any admissions of flaws suggests someone who might be so rigid that they cannot effectively attract other sheep who are not like them.

Ed and Charlotte, Tim and Carole are all examples of Wednesday Sheep who might be recruited as leaders. The caveat is, of course, that others in the organization should also already recognize them as leaders. That can be seen through watching how others respond to any suggestions they make in informal groups or in meetings. If others just ignore their comments and go on with their agenda, the sheep have not recognized them as leaders. Keep in mind the concept of positional versus relational authority. If, on the other hand, they can influence the direction of conversation, giving them positional power on top of their relational power can enhance their effectiveness. People like Ed and Charlotte, Tim and Carole, are secure enough in themselves to listen to the shepherd's ideas, flexible enough to consider a new vision, and adaptable enough to manage their own anxiety during any change that takes place. Someone like Santini, however, would be more likely to drive people than win them. Anyone who has ever actually worked with sheep knows that driving sheep usually just scatters the sheep and seldom gets the flock going in a common direction without a lot of additional frantic work.

THE WEDNESDAY SHEEP AS SHEPHERD

Leadership and ministry in the Judeo-Christian tradition are both primarily relational in nature. Whatever the theological frame of reference of the particular faith tradition, ministry is essentially about bringing people into relationship with God and into relationship with each other. As Peter said, "Once you were not a people, but now you are God's people" (1 Pet. 2:10). It follows, then, that just as not all sheep can be sheep-leaders of the flock, not all sheep are really fit to be shepherds. Those selected as shepherds should be at a very minimum of at least average relational and cognitive ability.

One quick disclaimer seems appropriate. In this chapter and in each succeeding one, we are assuming the validity of God's call to certain people. Each faith tradition has its own means for discerning who is truly called of God and who is not. Similarly, every organization has criteria for finding those best equipped to lead. The biblical witness is full of examples that God does not always choose the biggest and the best as leaders. Jacob, who was later known as Israel, was the younger of two brothers and such a dedicated con artist that even his name means "Trickster." David, the greatest king of Israel, was the youngest of seven brothers. Jesus' first four apostles were fishermen, and none of the Twelve were charismatic leaders. Today's business world is, likewise, filled with "unlikely" candidates who rose from very humble beginnings to achieve incredible success. We assume God can still call some seemingly unlikely people if God chooses to. This reality is the foundation on which all other suggestions are built.

The hundreds of interviews with candidates for ministry Wayne has conducted, as well as Chris' extensive research into the personality traits of successful leaders, show that there are some characteristics that a good Wednesday Sheep or shepherd ought to have. The would-be shepherd ought to give evidence of reasonably effective personal boundaries.[2] That is, the candidate should give evidence of some meaningful personal relationships. Wayne is fond of telling the candidates that he works with that every minister ought to have at least six close friends, otherwise six strangers will carry you to the grave. Some of these ought to be "parents," that is, older and presumably wiser people on whom the candidate can rely for experienced guidance. If the candidate's own literal parents are not available or are not suitable for any reason, the candidate should have ideally recruited someone "older" to fill this role.

This will help the candidate know how to recruit more experienced pastors to provide the mentoring the new shepherd will inevitably need starting out in the profession of ministry. Some of these close relationships ought to be peers. These will give the candidate experience in relating from a position of equality, where relationships have to be negotiated, not demanded or assumed. If there are areas where the candidate has cut off others or gives evidence of a "Lone Ranger" theme to his life, this may be problematic for the shepherd in building cooperative relationships within the church. The opposite extreme of excessive neediness is just as potentially damaging.

The candidate should also give evidence of a reasonably good ability to self-soothe anxiety as it comes. This is very high on the list of needs, and, based on Wayne's research, it is one that most candidates are likely to lack.[3] Many shepherds come into leadership with a higher-than-average need for external affirmation. They are particularly warmed by others' approval and sensitive to others' indifference. As any experienced shepherd knows, it is difficult if not impossible to keep all the people happy all the time. The shepherd will need the ability to manage that inevitable anxiety without falling into the temptation to use some sort of externals (for example, substance abuse, affairs, overwork) to manage it. Yet the research clearly suggests that shepherds are more likely than the average person to feel the need to use some sort of externals to manage anxiety.

Having been in personal counseling previously should not, in our opinion, be considered a negative when it comes to shepherd-candidates. Indeed, a positive experience of being "on the couch" can be a real asset when it comes to understanding the benefits that counseling can bring to sheep with whom the shepherd will work, and thus can potentially enable the shepherd to be more effective in relating to the sheep. What seems to be crucial is that the candidate who has been in counseling is able to articulate some benefits he or she gained from the experience.

With or without prior experience of having been in counseling, another key way this ability to self-soothe becomes necessary is the often competing demands of our current world. Many professional positions, and ministry especially, are extroverted professions. That is, they depend upon contact with others. There are very few jobs on earth in which a person can operate in complete isolation. Naturally, then, the true extrovert will find all the interpersonal demands energizing and thus will take to them more naturally. Other parts of every job, however, are very introverted. In ministry these introverted aspects include private prayer, sermon preparation, and Bible study. The person who is energized by interpersonal activities will find these introverted activities a drain, and the person who enjoys the introverted demands will find the extroverted activities a drain. The shepherd's ability to manage his or her own anxiety will enable the shepherd to strike an effective balance between the introverted and extroverted demands, without resorting to an either/or position.

Like all Wednesday Sheep, shepherds who are Wednesday Sheep are open to growth and change. Like all Wednesday Sheep, there are variations in their degree of openness and ability to change, but it is there. Change in the real world is seldom linear. Most often, it is "two steps forward, one step back." Nevertheless, the healthy leader, like all healthy Wednesday Sheep, will evidence a lifelong commitment to growth relationally and spiritually.

WHEN A WEDNESDAY SHEEP NEEDS HELP

In the last section of each of these chapters on the different types of sheep you might lead we are going to speak specifically to pastors. That said, all leaders may find this section useful in helping them understand what is going on within their organization. An injured sheep slows up the entire flock. If someone in your flock is not managing life well, that situation will reduce the person's effectiveness and efficiency within your organization. Knowing how to spot symptoms and possibly encourage the affected person to get the help he or she needs can go a long way towards helping you maintain the environment you want.

As a pastor, in understanding how to protect, feed, and lead your sheep you need to know when they are hurting and when they need help beyond what you can give. A shepherd who tries to provide help he or she is not trained to give will only end up causing the sheep further harm. So the question arises, when does a sheep need help that the shepherd cannot give?

Most Wednesday Sheep who require focused counseling or care need only very brief interventions. Again, based on our own research, most clergy candidates are truly caring individuals. That caring ability faithfully embodied by the pastor, combined with the power of God, can help the pastor be effective in many situations. As a rule of thumb, the pastor should devote a maximum of three fifty-minute sessions for any individual or couple.

The reasons for that rule of thumb are both practical and theoretical. From a practical perspective, the pastor just has too many components in his or her job description to devote the large blocks of time necessary to do good therapy. There are people to be visited, sermons to be prepared, worship services to be readied and led, committees to be organized and run, and community activities to be attended. Of course, this list does not include the pastor's own personal study and devotional time, family time, and so on. Just from a time management standpoint, the pastor who devotes hours each week to counseling is neglecting other essential duties.

The theoretical reason for the three-session limitation has to do with our ethical obligation to avoid exploitative or potentially harmful relationships. To see why this is a risk, take the example of Pastor Don. Don found he really enjoyed counseling and he had even taken some course work in pastoral counseling. When Lucy, the chair of his financial committee, started having marital difficulties, Don suggested that she and James, her husband, come in for marital counseling. They agreed to do so, and slowly Don was able to help them begin to heal some of their long-standing problems. After about six weeks, however, Lucy presented a proposal during the finance committee meeting with which Don totally disagreed. He tried to gently express his opinion, but Lucy held fast. Don knew from his counseling relationship that this was Lucy's pattern in her marriage—she tended to make a snap decision and hold fast to it regardless of the opposition. This knowledge put Don into a dilemma. If he revealed what he knew in order to sway the committee against Lucy's proposal, he would be violating a confidence (always ethically wrong), likely jeopardizing his counseling relationship with Lucy and James, and potentially damaging their willingness to participate further in church activities. They might even leave the church and take some of their friends with them. On the other hand, if he said nothing, he risked having a proposal he truly believed to be harmful for the church passed by the committee. Then he would have to go back to his counseling relationship with Lucy and James as though nothing had happened, when in fact he would be very frustrated. Either way, a barrier would be in their relationship that otherwise would not have been there.

Don should have listened to his sheep more carefully before he asked Lucy to chair the finance committee. He probably would have heard stories, usually told as funny stories, about some of Lucy's impulsive actions in the past. Even though she was a investment broker and was highly competent in the field of finance, the themes in her life story would have suggested that other Wednesday Sheep would have been more suitable for such a responsible position. Once she was in that position, however, if Pastor Don had simply listened to Lucy and James long enough to make an appropriate referral, he could have avoided the dual relationship and thus the dilemma he put himself in.

So how does the pastor know when to refer Wednesday Sheep? Again, any time the counseling relationship looks as though the presenting issue will not be resolved within three sessions, the pastor should refer. The one major exception to this rule of thumb is premarital counseling, which, by its very nature, often requires more than three sessions yet does not usually create an unacceptably high risk of a harmful relationship. Any time Wednesday Sheep show a major change from their previous level of functioning, a referral may very well be appropriate.

Finally, the Wednesday Sheep who is a shepherd should also be ready to make a self-referral. Brother Bob found this out when he responded to a middle-of-the-night call to the local hospital. Bill, one of his staunchest members, had been severely beaten during a robbery. Seeing Bill there in the hospital room opened Bob's floodgates of memory. He reexperienced the time when he was in high school and a gang of bullies had beaten him badly enough that he had to be hospitalized. While Bob was able to minister effectively to Bill's family that night, he found he was unable to sleep the rest of that night. All the next day, he was restless and unusually irritable. Clearly, he had been affected. Fortunately for his congregation, Bob was smart enough to call a therapist to whom he had referred many others and ask for an appointment for himself. In just a few sessions, Bob was able to work through his painful memories and return to his previous level of functioning.

This is the key to remember about Wednesday Sheep. While all humans are vulnerable to emotional, spiritual, and relational difficulties due to this being a fallen world, Wednesday Sheep function well enough that they usually are able to bounce back quickly, especially with appropriate professional help. How quickly? Several national surveys suggest that Wednesday Sheep will only need six to ten sessions with a competent therapist. As the case of Don, Lucy, and James illustrates, Wednesday Sheep are far from perfect. What distinguishes them from the other kinds of sheep in the fold is that they have enough resources that they only need a little outside help to be able to function well enough. Perfection will just have to wait for heaven.

Living into the Lesson

1. Given the description of the Wednesday Sheep, do you feel the majority of people within your flock fit the "normal" definition?
2. What "rules" have you had to adjust in your leadership style as you moved from flock to flock, or as you matured as a leader? How well have you adjusted to the new "rules?"
3. When have you not been able to adjust to a change? How did that inability impact your life and leadership?
4. What have you found helpful in leading Wednesday Sheep through transitional times? Talk to other shepherds and see what has been most effective in their ministry or leadership.
5. Give an honest self-analysis of how well you handle crisis leadership. How well do others think you lead in a crisis? Where do you most need to improve?
6. How have you done at making sure you have close relationships? Can you identify three to five close friends who are equals as well as one to two mentors with whom you share on a regular basis? If not, what steps do you need to take to find these relationships? What's holding you back?
7. How well do you manage your own anxiety? What do you have in place to help you "vent" when you feel stressed or anxious?
8. Have you been able to abide by the three-session rule in the past when counseling your flock? If not, why have you decided to do more? What do you believe is helpful about handling the counseling sessions yourself rather than referring?

4

MONDAY SHEEP

A pessimist is one who makes difficulties of his opportunities and an optimist is one who makes opportunities of his difficulties.

—HARRY S. TRUMAN,

THIRTY-THIRD PRESIDENT OF THE UNITED STATES OF AMERICA

Back in the 1966, the group The Mamas and the Papas had a big hit called "Monday, Monday," which spoke of how Monday was a day that would always turn out badly.[1] You could just count on it happening. That is the theme song of the Monday Sheep. The Monday Sheep cannot trust Monday, or any other day of the week. For them, this world is a dangerous place with hidden, unseen predators lurking behind every rock and tree. And there is very little they can do about it. Things will just turn out badly no matter what.

CHARACTERISTICS OF THE MONDAY SHEEP

Before we begin to describe Monday Sheep, allow us a word of clarification about this chapter. There does not appear to be a significant gender difference between the number of male and female Monday Sheep, and for that reason we will sometimes use male pronouns and sometimes female. The characteristics attributed to Monday Sheep of one gender applies equally well to Monday Sheep of the other gender.

To understand the spiritual perspective of the Monday Sheep, imagine, for example, that you have just preached a sermon addressing the concept of the believer's responsibility to help others, to be active in the church, and to give financially. What does the Monday Sheep in the congregation tend to hear? Regardless of what you actually said, the Monday Sheep hears you saying that now God, too, wishes to keep him working on the chain gang. He has to tend to the needs of his neighbor and never get around to having any happiness that is just for himself. On top of that, he is supposed to be joyful about all of this. It is as if God is saying to him, "Board this ship. Climb the gangplank, descend to the lowest galley, find your row and seat, close the shackles around your ankles and wrists, wrap your palms around the oar, and put your back into it. And it will be this way forever."

In his most soul-searching moments, the Monday Sheep might recognize that he envies worldlings because they do not seem to have to live under this miserable load. And since he himself does not find this way of life fulfilling, despite his tightly held belief that he is "supposed to," he may wonder why any unbeliever should be attracted to it either. Consequently, he may share his faith unenthusiastically or not at all. By using the law and guilt for motivation, the Monday Sheep can get himself to labor like a workhorse for God, but this approach hardly results in the Monday Sheep experiencing spiritual wholeness or joy. When you hear a sheep bleating about nothing but law, guilt, and obligation, you're dealing with a Monday Sheep. The Monday Sheep approaches every day as if it is Monday and as Garfield, the famous cartoon feline, is fond of saying, "I hate Mondays."

The problem is, up to a certain point, being a Monday Sheep can be quite rewarding, and that is what makes it so hard for the Monday Sheep to want to give up the shackles of obligation. Every organization loves people who will always follow the rules. They seldom cause problems for the organization, and their heavy burden of guilt means that they will gladly take on all the load that someone may choose to put on them. The Monday Sheep can tell herself that she is invaluable to her church (or her family, job, or civic group)—and she will be mostly correct. She has, by her hyper-responsibility, made herself that way. So while the Monday Sheep may inwardly complain about the load she carries, the Monday Sheep makes sure that no one deprives her of the pleasure of others' admiration for all her hard work.

Moreover, the rewards Monday Sheep receive are not just internal. Monday Sheep tend to earn promotions in business because they are more than willing to volunteer for extra projects, put in extra time, and pay extra attention to detail. It is not much of a leap of logic for Monday Sheep to believe God looks at them precisely the same way. The wise shepherd will have to watch for these tendencies, because the Monday Sheep, initially, can be just the person the shepherd is looking for. They never say no, they always work hard, they are always present, and they do the jobs they are given very well.

If anyone ever deserved the title "workaholic," it is the Monday Sheep, at least at the higher-functioning range of the continuum. It is not that the Monday Sheep enjoys work or finds it exciting and fulfilling. It is a compulsion. Work is something done to keep something else truly awful from happening. And here's the danger that can come back to bite the shepherd who is not aware of his or her flock. The Monday Sheep does not serve God, church, or job out of a sense of loyalty, love, or calling, but out of a sense that if they don't then something really bad will happen to them. The Monday Sheep may not know what that awful thing might be, but in her soul of souls, she is convinced that it will be as terrible as being eaten alive, and perhaps worse than that. Spiritually, the Monday Sheep knows that if he does not follow every rule, the flames of hell are just a heartbeat away. The eighteenth-century preacher Jonathan Edwards powerfully expressed the Monday Sheep's spiritual fear in his sermon "Sinners in the Hands of an Angry God."[2] The Monday Sheep believes he is like a spider being dangled from its web over a flame, a flame that threatens to break the web and doom the spider to torment at any moment.

Of course, the Monday Sheep would never admit any of this, often not even to himself. Especially in interactions with others, the Monday Sheep knows the rules say that he is supposed to find joy in serving others, so that is the language the Monday Sheep will use in talking about all he does. In other words, the Monday Sheep will use much the same language as the Wednesday Sheep, but by listening thoroughly, the shepherd can discern the difference. For the Wednesday Sheep, rules are guidelines that make life easier. For the Monday Sheep, the rules are invariant paths that must be followed to avoid destruction. For the shepherd, the big clue is that the Wednesday Sheep is able to negotiate rule changes when necessary. The Monday Sheep will change rules only with difficulty, if at all.

The same "my way or the highway" approach applies to the Monday Sheep's relationships. The Monday Sheep operates from an "I'm not okay, you're okay" position. This may be hard for others to see, because the Monday Sheep often comes across as very self-assured. This seeming self-assurance, however, is in reality an overcompensation for the feelings of anxiety and inferiority the Monday Sheep feels. The clue for the shepherd is that the Monday Sheep will seldom admit to the normal foibles of human life. Another clue is that the Monday Sheep will often become angry when others do not do what they are "supposed" to. This is in contrast to the Wednesday Sheep, who can accept mistakes and differences and take them in stride, while still trying to improve herself.

Often, Monday Sheep come from families where love was very conditional. They learned early and well that following the rules was the sole means of "earning" love, and love must be earned anew every day. If they violated the rules, they were not only disciplined, they also were treated as "gentiles and sinners" (to use a New Testament metaphor) in the family until they again "earned" their place. Another common path to becoming a Monday Sheep is recovery from substance abuse or any other lifestyle that the Monday Sheep now considers to be particularly "sinful." Tightly following the rules may well have been the way out of self-destruction at the time, but now the cure has become part of the problem. The Monday Sheep will say in essence, "Yes, see, I was terrible back then. But now God has changed me and now I am whole" (read, without flaw). A Wednesday Sheep experiencing the same sort of dramatic conversion might say, "Yes, I was terrible back then, and God is still working on me. I'm growing in God's grace." That is a subtle but significant difference.

Alice was a Monday Sheep in Brother Sam's congregation. Sam often overheard Alice talking to her girlfriends during fellowship times about Chad, her husband, and how he "always" ignored her. She felt like nothing more than a "maid with sex privileges," according to what she told her girlfriends. Not long after one of these times, Alice came into Sam's office to complain about others on the kitchen committee. Although she was not the chair of the committee, she had taken it on herself to organize a cleaning schedule, a schedule that others on the committee promptly ignored. Alice was hurt and angry that she felt she had to do everything herself, and she wanted Sam to tell the others on the committee to "live up to their responsibility. After all, it's our church, and we need to take care of it."

Such comments are very seductive because there is an element of truth to them. Committees do need to properly function if the church is to carry out its total ministry, even "behind the scenes" committees like a kitchen committee. If Sam had responded to Alice's overt request, however, he would have allowed himself to get pulled into her game, which would be a lose-lose position for him. If he responded by ignoring Alice, she would have become angry with him, too—just as she already was with Chad and the other members of the kitchen committee. This would also violate a major principle of leadership, which is you never ignore your flock. If Sam had responded by trying to get the other members of the kitchen committee to follow Alice's schedule, he would have reinforced for her that running to him is the way to solve problems, ensuring that the next time someone in the church did not do what they were "supposed" to, Alice would be right at Sam's door again.

Alice illustrates the overcompensation so typical of Monday Sheep. She appeared self-confident and self-assured, to the point of being able to demand from her husband and others that they do what they are "supposed" to do. But back stage, where even Alice could not see it, was her belief that she is not okay. Her rigid following of the rules was her way of compensating for her basic feelings of inferiority. Rather than trying to grow and overcome the inferiority, as a healthy Wednesday Sheep would, Alice, as a true Monday Sheep, tried to pull others down to her level of legalism. This is because, back stage, she believes that she needs to be taken care of and that others, who are more okay than she is, can take care of her if only they will. When she does not receive the levels of care she is "supposed" to, she feels perfectly justified in becoming angry.

Tragically, although Monday Sheep truly want close, intimate relationships, they seldom find genuinely intimate relationships. Their back stage anxiety prompts them to structure their relationships so that others cannot get close enough to see how truly "not okay" they are. Of course, if others cannot get close enough to see how "not okay" the Monday Sheep is, they also cannot get close enough to truly support the Monday Sheep. The resulting surface relationships serve as still more evidence to the Monday Sheep that they are not okay. After all, their unacknowledged, yet pervasive, logic goes, if I were really okay, people would love me the way I want to be loved. Since I do not feel loved "enough," I must be not okay.

LEADING THE MONDAY SHEEP

Although Monday Sheep will be a minority percentage of most congregations, they will consume a large amount of the pastor's time, as Sam's experience with Alice illustrates. Since Sam knew the principles of leadership in this book, he was able to respond to her more helpfully than if he had allowed himself to play her game. Sam listened carefully. He responded with empathy, not only to her overt messages but also to the covert themes he was hearing: "Alice, I am really impressed with how much you care about this church. You really put a lot of yourself into anything you do, even jobs that most people wouldn't appreciate, like being on the kitchen committee. You and I both understand that we couldn't have the great Wednesday night fellowship suppers we do if it weren't for you and the other members of the committee. You really make a lot of the good things around here possible, and I appreciate that. And I hear from you that following the rules is a very important part of what enables you to do all you do."

Giving a Monday Sheep this kind of response can often be very difficult for a shepherd. The Monday Sheep can be one of your hardest working, most responsible sheep. Many leaders recognize that today's society is very consumerist: "If I don't get what I want at your church, I'll just go down the street." The fear of losing a good worker can cause shepherds, both in the church and the corporate world, to go out of their way to appease the bleating of the Monday Sheep. The wise leader, however, will be able to act as Sam did and respond to the situation rather than reacting to it.

Sam stayed focused on his overall mission as leader while still being able to help Alice.

Sam's response also gave Alice part of what she needed and wanted—some external affirmation. Monday Sheep have very little ability to self-soothe, so what they most need when they are bristling like a porcupine is to have someone soothe them. Of course, when they are bristling, the last thing most people want to do is to get close enough to soothe, which just keeps the "I'm not okay" belief pattern going for the Monday Sheep. It takes a healthy Wednesday Sheep like Brother Sam, one who has the ability to calm his own anxiety in the presence of an angry member of his flock without dismissing her, to be able to listen closely enough to hear the hurt and fear underneath the anger.

After listening to Alice confirm that he had heard her correctly and had correctly spoken her inner beliefs, Sam went on to express his confidence that Alice would be able to work out the problem with the committee herself. Together they worked out a plan of action for Alice to carry out. They spent a few minutes rehearsing her contacts with other committee members, and Sam was able to help her refine her approach so she would be more likely to actually receive the response she wanted. Then Sam thanked her for her concern and suggested she call some time next week for an appointment the week after that when they could discuss her success.

Sam did a number of things correctly in being a shepherd leader to Alice. He put the responsibility for solving the issue back on Alice where it rightfully belonged. At the same time, he expressed his belief in her ability to carry out her plan, thus giving her more of the external affirmation she needed. Knowing that Monday Sheep tend to unconsciously put others off by their approach, he practiced with her and mentored her in expressing her concerns so that others would be more likely to hear the good parts of her issues without being put off by her style. Finally, he set some appropriate limits on interruptions of his time by asking her to make an appointment to see him, rather than just dropping by as she had this time, and to make the appointment for several weeks in the future. Pushing the appointment into the future further communicated confidence in Alice's ability, and communicated covertly, "I care about you but I am not going to be overwhelmed by anxiety over this issue. Because I can contain the anxiety, you can contain the anxiety."

Another way the shepherd can effectively lead Monday Sheep is by preaching sermons that appropriately balance law and grace. Saint Paul's letters in the New Testament provide a prime example of how to bring off this balance. For example, he wrote, "For through the law I died to the law, so that I might live to God" (Gal. 2:19). Paul dealt with a lot of Monday Sheep in Galatia. He was writing to people who believed that one must keep the letter of the law before being able to experience the grace of God. In this context, he explicitly taught that the law was a good gift of God, and that it faithfully pointed the way of righteousness. His emphasis on grace, however, came from the reality that the law could point the way to righteousness but not provide the power to reach it. That is why grace is necessary. In the shepherd's sermons, it is of course appropriate to highlight moral law, but always to emphasize that success in following the law never comes solely from our own effort, no matter how diligent, but always comes from our effort as empowered by the grace of God. As Proverbs 3:34 says, "Toward the scorners he is scornful, but to the humble he shows favor." Indeed, the Bible is full of stories of women and men who were selected by God for greatness despite their imperfections. Monday Sheep will have a hard time with that concept because they experience love, including God's love, as very conditional. Precisely for that reason, they need to hear it repeatedly. Sooner or later, it will begin to sink into their back stage, where it can do some good in actually changing their behavior.

Earlier in this chapter, we noted that being a Monday Sheep is functional up to a point, and that is true. When crises come, however, things can unravel very quickly because of the Monday Sheep's rigid following of one way of living. An illustration Wayne sometimes uses with his therapy clients may be helpful here: In almost all forms of martial arts, the student is taught to stand with the knees bent and the feet shoulder width apart. This is a very solid stance that allows the student to move quickly in any direction to meet whatever attack may come their way. That is the stance of the healthy Wednesday Sheep—a stance that enables them to move and adapt to almost any situation without becoming totally overwhelmed. By contrast, the stance of the Monday Sheep would more closely resemble the position of attention learned in the military. At attention, one stands rigid, knees very slightly bent, heels together, with toes pointed at a forty-five-degree angle from each other. It is a very solid position, and one can stand in that position for long periods of time without moving. Everyone who has ever been in the military has done it. Yet it is very hard to move from that position without a major upset. In fact, that is the point of being placed at attention—one is not supposed to move. The Monday Sheep is like that—solidly functioning as long as their tightly held rules work. Should life demand they move from this solid spot by changing their rules, they are likely to find themselves face down in the dirt.

This is because the Monday Sheep's response to a crisis is to do more of the same that they were doing before the crisis. Remember that the Monday Sheep chose his or her rules because the rules work to keep the much feared anxiety at bay—or at least in the shadows of life, where they do not have to be faced. This is why allowing a Monday Sheep to assume a position of power in a congregation is so risky. In a crisis, the Monday Sheep will continue to do what has worked in the past to keep her own anxiety in check, regardless of the evidence that others do not find this helpful and regardless of the evidence that some other procedure might even be better for the Monday Sheep. The more the Monday

Sheep feels pressure to change, the more tightly the Monday Sheep will cling to the old ways, because deep down he believes "I'm not okay, and therefore any change I make will inevitably be worse than what I now have."

For example, if the church is starting to have financial problems (and the astute shepherd will definitely notice this response in the business world, as well), the first response of the Monday Sheep might be to want the pastor to preach more about tithing. The Monday Sheep will use every opportunity to bring up how one "ought" to tithe and will talk disparagingly of those who do not tithe like he does (he will be sure to let you know that *he* tithes—he's doing it "right"). The Monday Sheep will block any attempt at a solution to the financial problem that does not fit his idea of the "right" way to handle things, and the more others try to reason with the Monday Sheep, the more the Monday Sheep will respond with anger. Those who do not see things his way are just being totally unreasonable, from his point of view.

Shepherds leading a Monday Sheep in a crisis will have to constantly reassure the Monday Sheep that the shepherd thinks they are just fine, even during this crisis time. They, the Monday Sheep, will require a lot of "cheerleading" for their efforts to cope. Often, this will take the form of what therapists call normalizing: "Joe, I think you're doing great in this situation. Almost anyone would be feeling overwhelmed in a situation like this, and I am impressed that you are doing as well as you are. What are you doing that is actually helping you do as well as you are?" In this situation the shepherd has helped the Monday Sheep realize, even if subconsciously, that what he is experiencing is "normal" and the shepherd has affirmed how well the Monday Sheep is handling the situation. At the same time, the shepherd will have to gently guide the Monday Sheep to create a new set of rules to deal with the crisis situation. Certainly, part of this will be to help the Monday Sheep seek help and support from others. Here, too, the shepherd's listening skills are crucial. Remember, to a Monday Sheep the close proximity of others represents an increased threat. Therefore, the pastor will need to draw upon the Monday Sheep's stories about dealing with past situations and the people who were, in the Monday Sheep's estimation, helpful during those past times. Only then can the shepherd begin by using the Monday Sheep's own list of resources, human and material, to help the Monday Sheep put resources together in new ways to meet the current crisis.

Even when the Monday Sheep explicitly asks the shepherd to "fix" the problem, as Alice did of Brother Sam, the Monday Sheep is still trying to be in control out of fear of the "what if I am not in control" that is always lurking on the back stage. In these cases, the Monday Sheep is really expressing control by saying, "Fix this. And you better do it right—or else." That is why, whether the Monday Sheep's crisis results in an explicit request for help or in a more private clinging ever more tightly to the old rules, the wise shepherd will work to calm his or her own anxiety before engaging the Monday Sheep. Only then can they jointly construct a solution to the problems that still keeps the responsibility with the Monday Sheep.

We should note, at this point, that sometimes entire congregations or businesses can function as a Monday Sheep (or any of the sheep styles). A normally healthy congregation, faced with a crisis (such as the financial crisis previously mentioned) or a drastic change (such as starting a new service or releasing a new product line) may suddenly start clinging to the old ways and rules, even if many of the individuals support the changes. It is important for the wise shepherd to diagnosis both the whole and the parts when deciding how best to lead. How the shepherd leads the entire flock may vary from how the shepherd leads the individuals within the flock.

One additional style of effective leadership of Monday Sheep comes from the insights of Adlerian Therapy. In teaching how to raise children, Adlerians make a distinction between praise and encouragement. Praise is the external evaluation of one's performance. It is the parent, and by extension the shepherd, saying, "You did a good job." Praise can be a good thing. We all enjoy praise from time to time. The Monday Sheep, however, is totally dependent on praise, and, therefore, when that praise is absent, automatically feels rejected.

That is why shepherds should use encouragement much more than praise in dealing with Monday Sheep. Encouragement focuses on the person's effort, not on the end results. For example, when Wayne was in college the only C he earned was in college algebra. If you had praised that C, he would have laughed in your face. Everyone knows C is not that good. It is "average" level work, and for a student used to higher grades it is generally not acceptable. Yet he also knew that he worked harder to earn that C than he worked to earn an A in any of his other college classes. If you had used encouragement, it might have sounded something like this: "Wayne, you really put in some effort on that algebra class. You must feel very good about the effort you put in to earn that C." Wayne certainly could have agreed with that and would have appreciated your noticing. Monday Sheep, accustomed to and dependent as they are on others' evaluations, need to learn the skill of appreciating their own honest effort rather than discounting it as not "enough." This can be especially true in the work force where results are the focus much more than effort. If a shepherd leader wants to get the best effort out of a Monday Sheep, encouragement is the best tool. Encouragement helps Monday Sheep develop a more balanced, healthy focus on results and effort jointly, rather than their typical sole emphasis on others' opinion of their results. As Saint Paul said, "Not that I have already obtained this or have already reached the goal; but I press on to make it my own, because Christ Jesus has made me his own" (Phil. 3:12). That is encouragement personified.

THE MONDAY SHEEP AS SHEPHERD

Psalm 23 paints the ideal picture of the shepherd. The shepherd's job is to "oversee" the sheep—to literally look over them and beyond them to see the green pastures and still waters the sheep need to prosper and grow. Of course, this does not mean the good shepherd is careless about the dangers that may beset the sheep of his flock. Indeed, the shepherd is both present in the moment, guarding against unseen but potential dangers, and present in the future, looking ahead to what is better for the sheep. It is this both/and ability of the good shepherd that comforts the sheep and makes them want to follow the shepherd.

When Monday Sheep become shepherds, they are not able to handle the both/and of effective leadership. They are far too busy looking for wolves and bears and lions that surely are there to attack them or the sheep. Their first impulse is to immediately circle the wagons to prepare for the bad that is, inevitably, on its way. As a result, their version of oversight feels to the sheep much more like being driven than tended.

In dealing with the sheep in their flock, Monday Sheep who are shepherds will preach sermons that are heavy on law and guilt. Monday Sheep in the flock will appreciate this style of preaching, because it fits their idea of the way they already believe things are and the way they "ought" to be. Other sheep, however, will respond less positively. Some may react in a passive-aggressive fashion, simply doing what they want regardless of what the preacher says. Others may ignore all the "oughts" and participate in the parts of the church where they feel less bound. Still others will respond by drifting to the fringes of the flock, being tangentially related to the flock at best. These are simply suggestive of the range of possible options. What will be clear when a Monday Sheep is the shepherd is that the flock is stuck drinking the same water, eating the same grass. Change is simply too scary for the Monday Sheep shepherd.

Conflict is often present when a Monday Sheep is the leader. He or she often will not wisely pick the battles worth fighting. Everything must be the way he says it must be, or the Monday Sheep shepherd will feel the opposition as a threat and thus a righteous battle. This can be anything from the way the altar is arranged for worship to the number of hymns or songs within the service to whether people stand or sit during a given part of worship. Of course, Monday Sheep within the flock will have equally firm ideas of the way things "ought" to be, and when these competing "oughts" clash, as they inevitably will, conflict is the sure result because Monday Sheep, by definition, cannot negotiate their rules. Of course, Monday Sheep have learned to disguise the conflict just as they have learned to disguise the joyless nature of their spirituality, so to the outsider everything may appear normal. Only after getting to the inside of church relationships can someone see that relationships between shepherd and flock are somewhat like a bunch of porcupines in a cave trying to snuggle to keep warm against the cold.

Part of what makes this dynamic hard to see for both outsiders, including other shepherds, and for sheep of the flock is that the Monday Sheep shepherd often does appear self-confident. Her quick, decisive answer to every question can be very comforting and reassuring, especially in times of social turmoil and upheaval. When the sheep of the flock are feeling threatened, they naturally want someone to make them feel secure. The Monday Sheep shepherd can deliver that sense of security in a time of perceived threat. It is only when the threat does not respond to the shepherd's fixed set of rules, or when the sheep no longer feel threatened, that this style of leadership becomes apparent for what it truly is.

Should the Monday Sheep shepherd manage to become the senior pastor of a multiple staff church (or CEO/VP/manager in a multiple-staff corporation), those they lead will no doubt suffer, regardless of the type of sheep they may be. The senior pastor who is a Monday Sheep must always be in charge. He will seldom give the associate pastor an opportunity to preach, and almost never at the primary service. Even when the senior pastor has to go out of town, he will be more likely to invite a pastor from outside to preach the main service than allow the associate to preach. Although he would seldom admit it, the reason is the senior pastor fears his position might be upset if the flock were to like the preaching of his associate better than they like his. To guard against this possibility, he will invite someone to preach who could not possibly be a threat.

Similarly, in church business the senior pastor will always be in charge. Even when he allows the associate pastor to have some responsibility, every major decision must flow through the senior pastor. Nothing of any significance happens without his personal approval. Of course, this is well justified with various management theories that will sound reasonable enough. Depending on the church's religious heritage, it may also be justified theologically and biblically. Whatever the justification offered, the real reason is that the senior pastor who is a Monday Sheep must always think he is in control. That is the only way he can keep his anxiety within manageable bounds.

Pastoral counseling and leadership consultations from a Monday Sheep will both sound more like a parent directing a child than the skilled work Brother Sam showed with Alice. One of Wayne's seminary professors, Albert, told of an experience that happened to him when he was a young priest at an inner city church. A homeless man came into the church and wanted someone to talk with. As the junior person on staff, Albert was assigned. But Albert was, at the time, very much a Monday Sheep, so as the homeless man told his story his mind was running at full speed about the other, more needful things he "ought" to be doing. Finally, the homeless man could stand it no longer and said, "Young Sir, the least you could do is listen." But Monday Sheep-shepherds cannot really listen. Their inner world is too full of dangers and fears to allow them to make room for anyone else, so despite what they know, despite the training they may have received, despite what they may hold as a front stage belief, their actual behavior shows they must keep people at a distance. The best way to do this for Monday Sheep shepherds is act as though their job is to dispense all the answers that the flock may need, even if the answer given is not to the question asked. At least it keeps the flock from looking too closely and seeing the "not okay" interior under the strong, self-confident façade the Monday Sheep projects.

Pastors who are other types of sheep may also have some of these same characteristics. What is clear is that any pastor who must be in control all the time and who is heavily focused on law and obligation and guilt in his ministry is not a Wednesday Sheep.

WHEN A MONDAY SHEEP NEEDS HELP

Readers who are psychologically astute may have guessed correctly that Monday Sheep represent the nondiagnosable range of what mental health professionals term anxiety disorders. Anxiety disorders represent one of the largest categories of mental disorders in the United States. According to the U.S. Surgeon General and the National Institutes of Mental Health, some 16.4 percent of the U.S. population, or approximately 44.6 million people, will have a diagnosable anxiety disorder at some point in their adult lives.[3] These figures do not count the adolescents and children who have anxiety disorders. While exact numbers are hard to come by because all mental health experts agree mental disorders of all sorts in children are grossly underdiagnosed and therefore undertreated, it is safe to say that the prevalence of anxiety disorders in children and teens is at least as high as it is in adults.

There are many different types of anxiety disorders, and learning all the differences is really necessary only for mental health professionals. What the shepherd who is not a full-time pastoral counselor or therapist needs to know is that the Monday Sheep described here are relatively functional. That is, they can get along in everyday life, although with pain and effort. They will need referral when that ability to get along starts to break down and the pain of everyday living increases.

One great example of that breakdown would be Melvin, masterfully portrayed by Jack Nicholson in the 1997 movie *As Good as It Gets*. Melvin was a prolific and popular romance novel author. Yet his own life was shut up inside his tightly controlled world. He could go out to eat, but only at "his" table with his own, hygienically wrapped, plastic ware, and only if he were waited on by "his" waitress (Carol, equally masterfully portrayed by Helen Hunt). When he arrived for a meal and someone else tried to wait on him because Carol was not there, Melvin came unglued. He went to outrageous lengths, including hiring one of the best physicians in town to care for Carol's son, so that Carol could come back to wait on him as she was "supposed to." The movie clearly shows the difference between a Wednesday Sheep under stress and a Monday Sheep. Due to her son's illness, Carol certainly had a constrained life and had very limited ways of dealing with stress. Yet when Melvin offered her some assistance that mattered, she was able to blossom and become a fuller person again. That is a typical Wednesday Sheep reaction. By contrast, Melvin, as much as we grow to love him during the movie, is still locked into his world of fear. He reaches out as best he can, but in the end it is Carol who moves the greater distance.

People who, like Melvin, are unable to meet the normal obligations of life, or who are only able to meet those obligations with great difficulty (witness Melvin's having five locks on his apartment door, each of which has to be locked and unlocked in a set sequence every time he goes out the door), are in need of a referral. Likewise, people who are experiencing racing heart rates and exaggerated startle response for which there is no medical cause are in need of a referral. People who have been in life and death situations themselves, or who have witnessed others in a literal life or death situation, may very well be candidates for a referral. Of course, any time one of the flock says, "Shepherd, life has just become too painful for me and I don't know what to do," that is certainly time for a referral.

The good news is that not all Monday Sheep will require professional help, and those who do can be successfully treated. According to the U.S. surgeon general, most people diagnosed with anxiety disorders and properly treated will find their symptoms reduced by 40–50 percent.[4] That is often enough to allow them to function with significantly less pain and effort than before. Some, like Albert, may even be able to leave their days as a Monday Sheep behind. But the healing will not start, cannot start, unless the shepherd encourages such sheep by word and deed to get the help they need and deserve.

Living into the Lesson

1. When you preach or teach, do you factor in how the different sheep in your flock will hear the lesson? Do you try and touch on different response points for different personalities?
2. Have you encountered someone motivated by law or guilt? How did your interactions with them generally go?
3. Have you ever used law or guilt as a means of motivating your flock? Why or why not?
4. Do you prefer working with people who follow all of the rules, regardless of their attitude, or would you prefer someone who is more carefree but maybe not as careful about guidelines?
5. How do you deal with a person who refuses to admit his or her own shortcomings? Do you find it easier to approach this situation with an equal or someone under your authority? Why?
6. How do you express unconditional love and acceptance in your leadership? What can you do to more intentionally convey these concepts to a Monday Sheep?

7. Have you ever had a situation like that described with Alice and Brother Sam? How did you respond? Would you respond differently if you had it to do over?
8. Have you ever gone out of your way to please a "bleating sheep" for fear of losing that person? How do these situations generally turn out?

5

TUESDAY SHEEP

"Good morning, Eeyore," said Pooh.
"Good morning, Pooh Bear," said Eeyore gloomily.
"If it is a good morning," he said.
"Which I doubt," said he.

—A. A. MILNE
IN THE PERSONA OF EEYORE, DONKEY AND FAMOUS PESSIMIST

Many kids have passed the time traveling to camping trips singing a silly song with a chorus that went, "Same song, second verse (or fifth or tenth or whatever it was), could get better but it's gonna get worse." That song would certainly fit the Tuesday Sheep. While the Monday Sheep fears everything will turn out poorly, the Tuesday Sheep *knows* it will.

CHARACTERISTICS OF THE TUESDAY SHEEP

Tuesday Sheep tend to be female. Some research suggests, for reasons that are not completely understood, that women are about twice as likely to be Tuesday Sheep as men.[1] That said, men are by no means immune from becoming Tuesday Sheep. In fact, nearly everyone, male and female, will show some of the characteristics of Tuesday Sheep from time to time, and that is perfectly normal. What should be of interest to the wise shepherd is when these passing characteristics are not passing—they are a lifestyle. When you have a person who is seen to be very much like Eeyore, you have your first clue that you are dealing with a Tuesday Sheep rather than with a Wednesday Sheep who is just going through a hard time.

To understand the spiritual perspective of the Tuesday Sheep, go back to the hypothetical sermon in which you are addressing the concept of the believer's responsibility to help others, to be active in the church, and to give financially—the sermon the Monday Sheep heard as all law and obligation. What does the Tuesday Sheep in that same congregation tend to hear?

Regardless of what you actually say or how carefully you phrase things, the Tuesday Sheep, like the Monday Sheep, will hear words of law and obligation—but with a twist. For the Tuesday Sheep, it is as if God were saying, "You know all these words to be true. You know you ought to be doing all this. And you know you do not measure up. You are weighed in the balances and found lacking one more time." Helping one of your flock grow to their full potential when that person does not really believe in his or her own potential is one of the greatest challenges a shepherd leader faces.

You probably will never know the pain in the Tuesday Sheep's heart unless you listen very carefully to her actions as well as her words. She has learned to live with it as an ever-present companion, and besides, she learned very early that it is far safer to hide the pain. While the Tuesday Sheep is fully aware of how inadequate she feels, to reveal these feelings to others would, in her mind, confirm for them what they already suspect about this person. As Wayne's father (Chris' grandfather) was fond of saying, "Better to keep your mouth closed and let everyone think you're a fool than open it and remove all doubt." The Tuesday Sheep would fully embrace this motto and try desperately to hide the "real" person from all others.

Typically, Tuesday Sheep choose one of two strategies to hide how they really feel. One is to become as invisible as possible. Tuesday Sheep will be the ones who come to worship, sit down, go through the motions, and leave, with little more than the minimum necessary pleasantries. When you ask how they are doing the Tuesday Sheep will reply "great" with a big smile and try to blend back into the crowd. These Tuesday Sheep are among the people whose presence at worship you have to look at the attendance pad to confirm. They make that little of an impression. That is quite deliberate (though also probably quite unconscious) on their part. This does not necessarily mean the Tuesday Sheep is shy or a "wallflower." She is just very average and it is her being so average that enables her to blend so well as to become invisible.

This strategy often comes into play when the Tuesday Sheep is asked to take some form of leadership. She will sit on the committee, as asked, but will have very little to say on any issue, will vote with the majority, and will slip out as soon as the meeting is adjourned, leaving you wondering if she was really present in the first place. A good shepherd will wisely, but carefully, attempt to draw the Tuesday Sheep into conversation. If the leader pushes her too hard, forcing her to engage in conversation, she might disappear for good. Without intentionality on the part of the shepherd, however, she might as well not be there at all.

The other major strategy of the Tuesday Sheep is to be the "class clown." This is typically a male Tuesday Sheep defense, though some female Tuesday Sheep have been known to master the technique quite well. The "class clown" Tuesday Sheep is the one that everyone in the church knows. This person is usually loud, full of jokes, and has a ready laugh. Unlike the Wednesday Sheep who has an active sense of humor, however, the "class clown"

Tuesday Sheep uses the humor to keep from being known. The Wednesday Sheep's humor is often self-revealing. The Tuesday Sheep's humor seldom is. Instead, the Tuesday Sheep's humor may be stories about fictional characters, humor at others' expense, or humor about almost anything except the Tuesday Sheep himself.

Art was one such "class clown" Tuesday Sheep. As far back as anyone could remember, he had a razor-sharp wit and he used it freely. In school, he poked fun at teachers. In the military, he poked fun at his commanders. In his church life, he always regaled his Sunday school class with stories about his coworkers on the job. He always told his stories with a laugh, so it was hard for anyone to not get caught up and laugh along. So when Art was hospitalized with a "mental breakdown" shortly after his position was "outsourced" by the company he had faithfully served for more than twenty years, everyone was totally surprised. "Not Art! He always seemed to take everything in stride. I don't understand it." And that is indeed the tragedy that the Tuesday Sheep lives with. No one truly understands him.

Brenda, Art's wife, was another Tuesday Sheep, but her strategy was the exact opposite. She was quiet, seldom speaking in class or to anyone she did not know very well. With her select friends, she was fun to be around, but with all others, she was polite, pleasant, and merely part of the background, like the paint on the walls—something that everyone sees and no one pays any attention to. Everyone just chalked this up to her accommodation to Art's rather forceful persona, but in reality, her marriage to Art was no fluke. Tuesday Sheep frequently marry each other.

This is because the Tuesday Sheep believes in his or her heart of hearts, "I am definitely not okay, and I'm not sure about you." Like Monday Sheep, they probably grew up believing love was very conditional, even if that was never the intent of the parents. Unlike the Monday Sheep, however, they gave up even trying to do "enough" to earn love. They just resigned themselves to the fact that they will never be loved no matter what they do, so there is no need to even try. Of course, that means they will never be loved by God, either. They may talk about God's love, but in the Tuesday Sheep's subconscious the unspoken message is, "This applies to everyone but you. You can't be loved, not even by God."

This does not necessarily mean the Tuesday Sheep are in a loveless marriage. Their relationship will be surface, but not necessarily loveless. Tuesday Sheep may truly love their partner and may earnestly desire to be loved. Their inner reality, seldom revealed in their faces, might be analogous to the old story about people in Hell who are seated at a banquet table piled high with delectable food. Each person in this story has one hand tied behind his or her back, and the other hand tied to a three-foot long spoon. They can reach the food with the spoon, but cannot get it into their mouths, and so it will be for all eternity. Tuesday Sheep know the banquet of love is real and it is wonderful for those who can eat it. For them, however, the joy of love is always on the table but seldom inside their yearning, empty hearts.

That is why Tuesday Sheep often marry each other or choose friends who are also Tuesday Sheep. They unconsciously select a partner and friends who are willing to accept a very surface relationship. It does not matter which strategy they use to hide. They are both playing by the same rules. The name of the relationship game is, "Hide, but don't seek." Even in their dating, they will talk endlessly about surface things, they will do things together, they may share some laughs, but when it comes to being real and vulnerable, that is where the walls go up. Because they share the same basic rules of relationship, even though the relationship is not satisfying, it is at least comfortable, like an old, worn-out shoe. They trade satisfaction for safety.

The Christian apologist C. S. Lewis's novel *The Great Divorce* describes some Tuesday Sheep very well.[2] In this fanciful tale, some people in Hell wanted to see what Heaven was like, so they chartered the transportation and made the trip. But when they arrived, some found that even the grass of Heaven hurt their feet. These had to go back to Hell where they could be comfortable. They are the Tuesday Sheep. They are unhappy in Hell and they can't stand to even walk on the grass of Heaven. Another motto that fits the Tuesday Sheep so well comes from Maxie Dunnam, noted author and former president of Asbury Theological Seminary. During one of his chapel sermons at the seminary he commented, "Many people would rather stay in the hell of the known rather than risk the heaven of the unknown." For the Tuesday Sheep, even if they wanted to take the risk, they "know" they would be doomed to failure.

This is the same trait that religious leaders will notice in the Tuesday Sheep of their congregation. They are never happy. They may or may not openly complain, but either way, nothing is ever right. The songs are too contemporary or they are too traditional, the preacher preaches too long or doesn't preach long enough, the people in the congregation are too cold or they are too intrusive. Nor do Tuesday Sheep confine their unhappiness to their church life. Tuesday Sheep are not happy at work, though they will usually have a lot of reasonable-sounding excuses why they are not. The boss is incompetent (and they can give illustrations why), and their coworkers are lazy or stupid. Home life is no better for the Tuesday Sheep, though they seldom complain about this part of their lives. It might be too revealing, and "Thou shalt not reveal thy inner pain" is one of their prime "Personal Ten Commandments." The wise shepherd will hear this relational pain by watching the way the couple, or the family, interacts. There will be few, if any, of the normal signs of connecting—socially appropriate touching, eye contact, relaxed conversation, and so on. Tuesday Sheep will look more like mere acquaintances sitting side by side (if indeed they are sitting together) than a couple or family with a vital love connection.

One further word about Tuesday Sheep is appropriate. Some people who are just introverted Wednesday Sheep may keep to the background as firmly as the Tuesday Sheep. To make matters even more complicated, some Tuesday Sheep, particularly the "class clown" type, have learned to act like very strong extroverts. The difference between the introverted Wednesday Sheep and the Tuesday Sheep is the presence or absence of joy. Even the most introverted of us can experience real joy and when we do, we send out the "vibes" that are unmistakable to others, regardless of our outer reserve. Tuesday Sheep, by contrast, seldom experience real joy. Their laughter is hollow, and if the shepherd listens very closely, underneath the laughter is a note of disappointment. For the Tuesday Sheep, life is just one disappointment after another. To be open and vulnerable to others is to open the doors too wide and allow more hurt and disappointment to rush in, and that is too great a risk to bear.

LEADING THE TUESDAY SHEEP

Fortunately for the shepherd, Tuesday Sheep are a relatively small percentage of the population. Most estimates place them at about 15 percent of the population, which is approximately the same as Monday Sheep. Unlike Monday Sheep, however, they will usually make few demands on the shepherd for leadership or pastoral care. They already know nothing is going to turn out right, so there is no use to bring their problems to the shepherd. Like Eeyore in the Winnie-the-Pooh tales, they just plod along and eat the thistles life gives.

The exception to this general rule is that some Tuesday Sheep (a small percentage of them) display their gloom and despair by being irritable. They will be very vocal about their unhappiness with the way things are going. They may go directly to the pastor or, perhaps more likely, they may simply spread their discontent among their "inner circle"—those they have judged as "safe." As the old saying goes, even the devil can quote scripture, so every wise shepherd will always listen to complaints to see what, if any, note of truth they may contain. Then the shepherd can take action as appropriate. The clue, however, that the shepherd is dealing with a Tuesday Sheep is that the action, no matter how well performed, will not make a difference to the Tuesday Sheep. Something else will be wrong. By contrast, the Monday Sheep will be quite happy, as long as the change is "the right" change (in other words, the change they expect and want). The Wednesday Sheep can adapt to various ways of doing things without undue upset.

These irritable Tuesday Sheep will demand inordinate amounts of the pastor's time. Amy was one of these, and Rabbi Spiegel was about to pull his hair out. Amy had been a lifelong member of the congregation, and she was among those who were most faithful in her attendance at Sabbath services, as well as the various Holy Day services. Yet she was never happy. She never approached Rabbi Spiegel directly, but she had something negative to say about every Sabbath or Holy Day service. When she was in the hospital, Rabbi Spiegel called her to tell her he was out of town and could not personally come to see her but he was praying for her. When she was discharged from the hospital, Amy called all her friends to complain that the Rabbi never visited her. Yet when she saw Rabbi Spiegel during services, she was always polite and "proper." Knowing what he knew, this contradiction made it hard for the good rabbi to look forward to congregation activities where Amy might be present.

This is another clue that you are dealing with a Tuesday Sheep. Tuesday Sheep not only feel no joy or positive anticipation in their own lives, they also tend to suck the joy out of everyone else's lives. Astronomers have discovered a phenomenon in space they call "black holes"—sources of gravitational pull so intense that not even light can escape. Tuesday Sheep can be the black holes of your flock. The pull of their inner core of pain borne of negativity is so great that it sucks the joy out of everyone with whom they interact on more than a casual basis. One frustrating aspect to this is that

Tuesday Sheep can often be very thoughtful and have a lot to offer at work, church, or in a relationship. The problem is that they present their ideas in such a negative, defeatist attitude that no one wants to listen to them. As the saying goes, it's not what they say, but the way they say it. As a result of their presentation, even their good ideas are often ignored, which reinforces the perception of failure that the Tuesday Sheep always carries around.

As previously indicated, Tuesday Sheep tend to marry Tuesday Sheep, but this is not invariably true. Sometimes a Wednesday Sheep (or other type sheep) can get fooled by a Tuesday Sheep's protective exterior and only discover too late that they are in a joyless and/or unsatisfying marriage. Anyone who has ever had the responsibility of hiring for any job can relate to this dilemma. People can fool you during an interview, and Tuesday Sheep are exceptionally good at keeping their shortcomings initially hidden. Some lower functioning Wednesday Sheep may even knowingly begin a relationship with a Monday or a Tuesday Sheep in the mistaken belief they can "fix" them. Inevitably, these well-meaning souls eventually find that their partner's patterns are far too ingrained to be "fixed" through marriage.

The discovery will be no less painful for another Tuesday Sheep, but since life for them is just one series of disappointments, they reason, what's the difference? Other types of sheep are not so resigned. They are likely to respond to the gravitational pull of the Tuesday Sheep's negativity by putting more and more emotional distance between themselves and the Tuesday Sheep until finally the relationship is at a "safe" distance—that is, the relationship is only a surface relationship. But since most other sheep, for various reasons, typically are not satisfied with only a surface relationship, they are likely to divorce the Tuesday Sheep out of self-protection. Tragically, this just reinforces the Tuesday Sheep's already present belief that she or he is unlovable and therefore wise to keep the relationship at a surface level where the inevitable break will not hurt so badly, just like Eeyore when Pooh and the gang try to throw him a birthday party in "A Day for Eeyore." Even more tragically, the Tuesday Sheep, like Eeyore, continuously repeats the pattern unless a shepherd steps in and helps turn the Tuesday Sheep in the right direction.

Obviously, divorce was not an option for Rabbi Spiegel, since he was not married to Amy and he did not want to leave the congregation he truly loved. As a healthy Wednesday Sheep, he talked the situation over with several trusted colleagues, including the president of the congregation, who also knew Amy quite well and who had proven his ability to keep a sensitive confidence. Together they formed a plan they believed would help Amy and the congregation.

Rabbi Spiegel called on Amy at her house. After the usual pleasantries, he asked her if she would be a consultant to the Chanukah committee. At first, she tried to defer, but Rabbi Spiegel pressed his point. He pointed out the many years she had been active in the congregation and that she had, from a little girl forward, been part of the synagogue's Chanukah festivities. Furthermore, he provided her a detailed, step-by-step list of the areas where her expertise would be very valuable to the committee. Unknown to Amy, the president of the congregation had already asked his wife, who chaired the Chanukah committee, to "cheerlead" each success and each honest effort Amy made, while ignoring her inevitable irritable remarks. When Amy finally agreed, to her surprise, that year's Chanukah was one of the best ever. Rabbi Spiegel thought so, too, because for the first time in years, he was able to truly enjoy the celebration.

Rabbi Spiegel embodied several important principles in leading Tuesday Sheep. Regardless of which variation the particular person might represent, the shepherd never wants to put a Tuesday Sheep in charge. Most of the time, they will steadfastly refuse to accept positions of leadership. Even if they do accept a leadership role, they will be sure to snatch defeat right out of the jaws of victory. After all, they live with a story line that says they are unlovable, and therefore they can never do anything truly right. What Rabbi Spiegel did was to ask Amy to be a "consultant." The success or failure of the committee was not dependent on her. At the same time, her "consultant" role defused her ability to irritably complain without revealing to everyone how unhappy she truly is, and that, as already indicated, is one of the Tuesday Sheep's prime Ten Commandment—"Thou shalt not be self-revealing."

Another wise strategy Rabbi Spiegel employed was providing Amy a step-by-step list. This strategy directly targeted one of the main reasons that Tuesday Sheep are so unhappy. They are masters of "all or none" thinking. Everything must be totally wonderful or it is totally awful. Of course, since nothing in this world is ever totally wonderful, for the Tuesday Sheep it naturally follows that everything is awful. This same kind of all or none thinking gets applied in various areas of their life. They do not problem solve well, because for them, life "ought" to be like a TV show, where problems come, are solved, and go away all within the space of an hour. This is not a matter of intelligence, but of a particular style of thought dysfunction that is inherent in Tuesday Sheep.

For example, if you were to ask a Tuesday Sheep what happens when someone dies, the Tuesday Sheep will probably say something like, "Well, you have a funeral and they are buried." The Tuesday Sheep will have no idea about the multitude of steps involved in those two seemingly simple statements. That is what makes everything so overwhelming for them. Knowing this is how Tuesday Sheep think, Rabbi Spiegel gave Amy step-by-step procedures so she would not be overwhelmed.

The third thing that Rabbi Spiegel did right in ministering to Amy was to arrange for a cheerleader. Praise is very hard for Tuesday Sheep to hear. They are too accustomed to not receiving it, and therefore they are very good at deflecting it. Amy certainly fit that description, and Rabbi Spiegel knew that one positive experience was not going to make a major change in her. She was too comfortably miserable to easily move to being happy, even for a short while. Nevertheless, he also knew that praise for obvious accomplishments that comes from multiple directions, combined with ignoring the old behavior, would begin to chip away at the walls of misery. The armies of Israel marched around the walls of Jericho for six days, and seven times on the seventh day, before anything happened (Josh. 6). People like Amy have walls that are thicker and harder to breach than Jericho's.

Even so, the wise shepherd will not be fooled into thinking that the Tuesday Sheep is impregnable. Far from it. One good analogy is something often learned in martial arts training. One of the training methods often used is to stand for long periods balanced on one leg. The purpose of the exercise is to learn to control the body using a minimum of movement. When Wayne became a pilot, he had to stand on one leg for at least thirty seconds during each flight physical to demonstrate that his inner ear (and sense of balance) was normal. Standing on one leg is not a solid stance. It is possible to learn to balance on one leg, but if something happens that requires a quick response, you must either put down your other leg in order to meet the challenge or risk winding up on your face. The Tuesday Sheep is like that—except that putting down the "other leg" is not an option for them. They go through life balanced precariously on their few coping skills, praying that nothing, not even a gentle breeze, will push against them, yet convinced that, sooner or later, they will wind up face down in the dirt.

Tuesday Sheep like Amy are definitely the exception. Normally, the shepherd's opportunity to lead Tuesday Sheep will be limited to more public activities, such as Bible studies, worship services, and perhaps routine visits (such as might be appropriate before a confirmation or a bar mitzvah, for example). To best lead Tuesday Sheep, sermons (and this would apply to business plans as well) should be carefully prepared with very clear, behaviorally specified outcomes. For example, the preacher will not simply challenge people to become "better disciples," but go on to define precisely what one can do to be "a better disciple" (for instance, "pick one five-minute period during the week to have a prayer with your family" or "bring one can of food to the local food bank"). Bible studies that focus on the ways that biblical characters dealt with and overcame adversity will be extremely helpful to Tuesday Sheep. Jesus' disciples did not "get it" for three years, and they had to go through some pretty awful situations before they finally did "get it." Yet when they did, they "turned the world upside down." A Tuesday Sheep will find comfort in this type of example.

Leading a Tuesday Sheep does not strictly occur in a ministerial setting. You must also lead your Tuesday Sheep in committee meetings. Some of you reading this might be looking for advice on how to handle this type of person in the business world. The same principles apply no matter the situation. The leader must be very specific as to what he or she expects from the Tuesday Sheep. The shepherd must also learn to be a cheerleader while allowing the grumblings to go in one ear and out the other. Finally, the shepherd must intentionally seek to draw out the Tuesday Sheep, even when others would rather the Tuesday Sheep just go away.

George was an assistant manager at a rent-to-own business. One of his delivery drivers, Fred, was most definitely a Tuesday Sheep. Everything was wrong. The hours were bad, the company was bad, the kind of work you asked him to do was bad. If asked to "clean up the stock room" or do anything other than deliver something, Fred would complain nonstop. George and the store manager were ready to fire the guy. After some wise advice from a mentor, however, George changed tactics. He typed up a very specific to-do list for each day Fred worked. When the work was done properly, George went out of his way to cheer Fred on. He put Fred in charge of training new delivery guys. Very slowly, Fred became a productive part of the team. Tuesday Sheep can make a vital contribution to your flock, if you're willing to put in the time to help them.

THE TUESDAY SHEEP AS SHEPHERD

Despite their usual reticence to take leadership roles, some Tuesday Sheep will eventually become leaders. In their younger days, they may well have found the church was that one source of safety in another wise hurtful world and so becoming a pastor might hold a certain amount of appeal to them. Certainly, the church's message of unconditional love would be attractive, even if they have a difficult time accepting it for themselves. In any event, the church might look like a great place to hide. After all, their back stage logic will say, "I don't have to talk about me. I just have to talk about God. No one will care about me."

Of course, in order to be a leader and not just a boss requires a lot of relational skills. Being a pastor, especially in Protestant Christian denominations, is essentially a relational job—a fact that the Tuesday Sheep entering ministry does not count on. After all, the function of organized religion is to bring people into a relationship with God and with each other. Denominations may differ on how best to accomplish these twin aims, but these aims do cut across all the usual lines. Just as in all other relationships, the Tuesday Sheep finds that closeness is frightening, because closeness equates to being vulnerable. The seeming safety of a church vocation vanishes in the rough-and-tumble of everyday church life.

At best, this sudden realization will result in a shepherd who becomes a hermit in his or her own office. On the worse end, some Tuesday Sheep shepherds will respond to this crushing awareness of their own vulnerability by dropping out of professional ministry completely. This scenario adds another boulder to the load of "You're not okay" rocks they are carrying and entrenches them even more deeply as a Tuesday Sheep. Nevertheless, many will never admit the real reason for leaving ministry. As they always do, the Tuesday Sheep will have a very reasonable-sounding rationalization of why it was someone else's fault. Even if these rationalizations do not really convince anyone, they do serve their primary function—they keep the Tuesday Sheep from ever being truly known.

More Tuesday Sheep respond by hiding within the system. In our numerous years of professional ministry, we have witnessed this attitude many times. The Tuesday Sheep hiding within the system may preach sermons filled with lots of law and obligation, pouring onto others the self-condemnation the Tuesday Sheep feels but cannot admit. The Tuesday Sheep's sermon illustrations may contain unfavorable information about his own family or others in "another" church, but never about himself. Alternatively, the Tuesday Sheep will preach sermons that are full of pious platitudes that ultimately say nothing. Likewise, the Tuesday Sheep's Bible studies may be scholarly, they may be factual, but they will ultimately lead nowhere.

The entire organization, whether church or business, under the leadership of a Tuesday Sheep is usually just going through the motions. Relationships, human and spiritual, are kept on the surface. While attendance figures may not significantly change, there will be little or no real vitality in the church's spiritual life. Like the life of the Tuesday Sheep, everything is shown to be perfect on the outside, but is really dying on the inside. This concept brings to mind Jesus' accusation against the Pharisees that they were like "whitewashed tombs, which on the outside look beautiful, but inside they are full of the bones of the dead and of all kinds of filth" (Matt. 23:27). This is not to say all biblical Pharisees were Tuesday Sheep, but that Jesus' analogy is often very fitting for the type of leadership Tuesday Sheep demonstrate.

Typically, the Tuesday Sheep-become-shepherd will invest his (or her) vitality in denominational activities. If there is no denominational structure in which to hide, the Tuesday Sheep Shepherd will devote large amounts of time and energy to nondenominational organizations. Either way, the unspoken object is to keep the focus on some cause, rather than on the Tuesday Sheep her- or himself. That is the mark that distinguishes the Tuesday Sheep from the Wednesday Sheep who is just passionately dedicated to a cause. In listening to the Wednesday Sheep, you will hear some of her or his "self" coming through. You will seldom if ever hear "self" coming through the bleating of the Tuesday Sheep shepherd. Meanwhile, the local congregation the Tuesday Sheep shepherd supposedly serves will be going through the motions, looking good on the outside, but empty on the inside.

WHEN TUESDAY SHEEP NEED HELP

By now, the clinically astute reader will have surmised that the Tuesday Sheep embodies what mental health professionals call depressive disorders. The descriptions provided in this chapter illustrate the nonclinical range of depression. Tuesday Sheep in this range do function, but with an effort. It is as though they are walking through life with a twenty-five-pound pack on their back. While they could no doubt benefit from therapy (research suggests that 60 to 80 percent of even clinically depressed people can find significant symptom relief), they are not likely to ask for a referral or volunteer for therapy. After all, their core belief is that they are unlovable, so what, from their perspective, is the point of going through all that effort? Tuesday Sheep shepherds are not likely to refer others for the same reason—their own back stage belief that nothing ever really changes. For them, therapy is nothing more than "rearranging the deck furniture on the Titanic."

Likely, it is only when the weight of life increases to, say, a fifty-pound pack that the Tuesday Sheep is likely to ask for help. This is not a case for the average pastor. Once life has become painful enough or hopeless enough, suicide becomes a very real danger. In fact, when the shepherd is faced with a Tuesday Sheep for whom life has become too painful to mask or hide any longer, the shepherd should explicitly ask if she or he has thought about suicide, and, if so, if she or he has a plan and the means to carry it out. Do not worry about putting the idea into the person's mind. If they have not thought of it, your asking about suicide will not add to the risk. On the other hand, if they have thought about it and you do not ask, you could well be attending an unexpected funeral.

The research is very clear that some form of cognitive therapy is the treatment of choice for depression. Depressed people may well need psychoactive medication to be able to use talk therapy, but, despite what you may hear, there is no evidence that medication alone "cures" depression or is any better than talk therapy. Do refer to a competent mental health professional who is supportive of you and your religious beliefs, and who knows about the research on effective treatments of depression. Family therapy may very well be indicated because other family members may well have subclinical levels of depression (remember Tuesday Sheep tend to marry Tuesday Sheep, and simply living with a Tuesday Sheep is emotionally and spiritually draining).

Tuesday Sheep are not fun to have in the flock. But they are there, and some experts believe that their numbers, by percentage, are increasing. One probable reason why this is so is the illusions created by the media that things "ought" to be fixed quickly and when they are not, something is wrong.

A powerful illustration came from interviews with people following the devastation of Hurricanes Katrina and Wilma in 2005. Barely hours after a major hurricane had passed through their area, news reports showed people complaining that they didn't have power or water or air conditioning. They complained that they had to wait in lines for their necessities. Earlier generations, less accustomed to the instant fixes of "mess it up and fix it up all within sixty minutes" media programming, would have said instead, "Of course things are a mess. But I survived. I can cope with the inconvenience." When we tell ourselves that things "ought" to be better and they are not, we are thinking like Tuesday Sheep. Those thought patterns are becoming more common in our culture, especially among our teens. So the wise shepherd will learn to listen to the bleating of the Tuesday Sheep, and will learn from resources such as this how to minister to them.

One final word: If any readers recognize themselves as Tuesday Sheep, do yourself, your family, and your congregation a favor. Seek some help. You can reasonably expect that, with proper treatment, things can be noticeably better despite what you may have believed up to this point.

Living into the Lesson

1. Have you met someone in your flock with an Eeyore-type personality? What challenges arose from leading this type of person?
2. Do you look for the "wallflowers" in your flock? What do you intentionally do to engage them? What strategies have you found effective for drawing them out of their shell?
3. How do you respond to the "class clowns" like Art? Do they frustrate you or do you enjoy their company? How have previous attempts to shepherd this type of sheep gone?
4. How do you respond to a person who prefers a surface relationship? Do you allow the relationship to stay at the surface or do you try to force it to go deeper? How have past relationships with this type of person gone?
5. How do you respond to a person who comes to you constantly complaining? How have you been effective in the past leading this person? What have you done that was not so effective?
6. How effective have you been at setting boundaries with a member of your flock who demands an inordinate amount of time? What has helped or hindered you?
7. Do you generally give specific steps when providing instructions or do you give more of a "big picture" and allow people to work out the details on their own? When dealing with a Tuesday Sheep how can you intentionally be more specific in leading them?

6

BIRTHDAY SHEEP

Nobody can be kinder
than the narcissist while you react
to life in his own terms.

—ELIZABETH BOWEN, IRISH AUTHOR

Most everyone, especially children, looks forward to his or her birthday. Granted, as we get older we may fuss and complain about our age, but the day itself we look forward to. As a child there is something particularly magical about that day. Often it's the one day of the year when you can invite any friends you want to come to your party. You get to decide everything that happens at the party, including the menu—a very rare privilege for a child in some families. Your birthday is the one day of the year where it's socially acceptable to be completely narcissistic—everything centers on you. It can be great. Christmas is fun and magical, but it is shared by everyone. Your birthday is completely about you.

While many adults probably do not look at birthdays with quite the same degree of excitement and wonder that children do, there are sheep in every church's fold for whom every day is like their birthday. These are the Birthday Sheep.

CHARACTERISTICS OF THE BIRTHDAY SHEEP

While Tuesday Sheep tend to be predominantly female, our research suggests that about 50 to 75 percent of Birthday Sheep are males. Sadly, the reasons for this gender bias are no better understood than the gender percentages for Tuesday Sheep. Keep in mind that almost all teenagers, male and female, behave like Birthday Sheep. This behavior, while often frustrating to their parents, is perfectly natural at their stage of the life cycle. What is just as natural is that most people eventually mature, grow out of that stage, and become the typical Wednesday Sheep. Unfortunately, a certain percentage of the population does not, and these may become the Birthday Sheep.

To understand the spiritual perspective of the Birthday Sheep, let us return to the hypothetical sermon in which you are addressing the believer's responsibility to help others, to be active in the church, and to give financially—the sermon the Monday and Tuesday Sheep heard as all law and obligation. What does the Birthday Sheep hear?

On a conscious level, the Birthday Sheep hears praise for his dedicated efforts. Even if his eyes never move from the preacher, in his mind, he is scanning the congregation and mentally comparing himself to others—always favorably. "I give more than he does. I spend more time volunteering than she does. Those folks over there can't hold a candle to me in terms of my knowledge of the Bible." For the Birthday Sheep, the sermon will be a confirmation that he truly is superior. Likely, it will be hard for him to suppress a self-satisfied smile.

Back stage, however, so deeply hidden that not even the Birthday Sheep is aware of it, is a gaping emptiness. It is not the anxiety of the Monday Sheep or the painful, depressive pessimism of the Tuesday Sheep. It is a vast, barren desert of the soul that is so inhospitable that joy or pain or anxiety cannot grow there. Only emptiness. This creates serious leadership challenges for any type of shepherd, both in the workplace and in the church. For the pastor it also creates theological issues. How can you help someone achieve his or her full potential when that person refuses to admit the need for growth?

Perhaps a helpful analogy comes from Wayne's experience in the USAF. One of his duties during his year in Korea was to visit the U.S. troops stationed on the Demilitarized Zone (DMZ). During these visits, he could not help but notice the very impressive building just on the North Korean side. It was from this very impressive structure that the soldiers and diplomats came when official negotiations between North and South were to take place. Soldiers often marched smartly in formation out of this building to stand guard and try to intimidate the Allied forces. On one of his visits, however, the U.S. helicopter pilot flying him to his next assignment made a pointed observation. The pilot flew as close to the actual border as he could and had Wayne look out the open door. To Wayne's surprise, the very impressive North Korean structure was just a front—like the front of a building used in a movie set. Behind the impressive façade was nothing more than the necessary props to hold it in place. It was all show, and no substance. That is the life of the Birthday Sheep.

The tragedy is that most Birthday Sheep have no clue that this emptiness exists. To look at it would be far too devastating. It would for them be like Lot's wife looking back at the destruction of Sodom (Gen. 19:26). They are only aware of their front stage confidence and self-satisfaction.

Most Birthday Sheep are wise enough and have learned well enough to keep their display of self-confidence within acceptable limits. Indeed, they can be very hard to distinguish from genuinely self-confident Wednesday Sheep. To distinguish between the two, the wise shepherd will have to listen very carefully indeed—listen with all of the skills referenced in chapter 1.

Everyone likes praise, and good leaders always find a way to genuinely praise their followers. This builds morale among the flock and increases loyalty to the leader. When Chris was working on his undergraduate degree in meteorology he interned at a TV station where the chief meteorologist went out of his way to praise everyone he came in contact with—from the other anchors to the camera operators to the secretaries. No person went unnoticed. As a result, he was loved by everyone at the station. People worked better when he was around and he made the work environment a better place.

Not only is praise good for the church or workplace environment, by paying careful attention to the way the person being spoken to responds to the praise, the astute shepherd can often find a large clue as to the type of sheep he or she is dealing with. The Wednesday Sheep will accept the praise with socially appropriate expressions of humility. The Wednesday Sheep, however, is quite capable of functioning without the praise, as enjoyable as it is. The Monday Sheep will take praise as evidence that this particular behavior made the Monday Sheep loveable. As a result, the Monday Sheep's acceptance of the praise will appear to be at least a little out of proportion to the praise itself—"Methinks thou doth protest too much," as Shakespeare might have said.

The Tuesday Sheep will deflect the praise, often by changing the subject or pointing to someone else. Praise is too incompatible with the Tuesday's basic "I'm not okay" belief system. Praise is the very breath of life, however, for the Birthday Sheep. Outwardly, the Birthday Sheep will appear to take it with the same easy grace as a Wednesday Sheep. The real difference is the Birthday Sheep cannot function long in the absence of praise, and, even more telling, the Birthday Sheep cannot give honest praise. When it comes to praise for the Birthday Sheep, "give and take" means, "You give and I take."

Of course, since most Birthday Sheep have learned how to keep from being too obvious, they have developed subtle ways to mask their inability to give the praise they so desperately crave. They may, for example, praise others while also reflecting the praise back on them: "Yes, Bob has certainly done a great job. I'm really glad I hired him." Or even less subtly, "I taught him everything he knows." The Wednesday Sheep, of course, might have said the first sentence and left the second unsaid. For the Birthday Sheep, however, everything must reflect positively on him. Praise of others is only a subtle way of gaining praise for himself.

Teenagers in the United States, especially, show this characteristic easily. When a teen has a pimple, for example, the teen is absolutely convinced that even the smallest red blemish looks three feet tall to everyone else. After all, that is what the teen sees when he or she looks in the mirror—something that is impossible to miss. U.S. teens also show their "individuality" by dressing like everyone else in their peer group, or by playing the same music as everyone else in their peer group, or engaging in the same activities as everyone else in their peer group. Their dependence on external approval shows clearly in their changing their personality about as often as they change their clothes, which can often be several times a day. Again, all this is perfectly normal at their stage of the life cycle. They try on various external definitions of "me" until they find one that fits. Eventually the parts that fit become their core of "This is who I am," and the resulting inner story gives them a stable direction for the rest of their lives.

Pastors who shepherd teenagers need to be acutely aware of this issue, as the teenage years will set the tone for the faith narrative during the adult life. Intentional leadership is necessary to help make those core beliefs formed during the teenage years positive ones. We have heard many times the statistic that 90 percent of persons experiencing Christian conversion do so before age twenty-one. While we have not found a verifiable study to prove this statistic, we do not doubt its general accuracy. We would go so far as to say that 90 percent of people who become atheists also do so before age twenty-one, and the same for people who become Muslims, Buddhists, or any other faith system. Why? Because the teenage years are when the sense of self is formed. This is what makes intentional leadership so vital.

This lack of a stable sense of self is what makes teens so emotionally volatile. A teen can be happy and loving one minute, and raging or crying the next. Because they do not yet have a solid story of who I am, they have very little ability to self-soothe. Their emotions are highly reactive to whatever happens in the external world. This, also, is helpful to remember when trying to shepherd your teenage sheep. Their ability to feel emotions is just as developed as an adult's. What they have not yet developed is the ability to regulate those emotions internally, rather than externally.

Unfortunately, the Birthday Sheep retains these same typically teen characteristics throughout life. At the lower end of their functioning, they are as insufferable in their self-centeredness and egotism as teens at their worst. Few Birthday Sheep function at this level, however. The natural criticism they receive for such culturally unapproved self-centeredness is too painful to bear. Those Birthday Sheep who do function at this lower level are able to do so only through massive use of what psychotherapists call denial. Their unconscious, but still quite powerful, emotionally protective walls keep out the jabs of others and also keep them from ever truly connecting with others. They are incapable of genuine empathy.

Indeed, these lower functioning Birthday Sheep are very much like Narcissus in the Greek myth. Narcissus was a very handsome man, and the nymph Echo fell in love with him. Narcissus, however, totally rejected Echo. He was too aware of his own beauty to fool with someone as merely "average" (in his estimation) as she was. Echo was crushed, and she faded away to a mere shadow of herself—the reflected sound we hear when we yell into a mountain valley, perhaps. The gods were so angry at Narcissus that they condemned him to do more of what he was already doing—when he passed by a pool, he saw his own reflection in the water and immediately fell hopelessly in love with the reflection in the water. There he sits for all eternity, gazing lovingly into the face in the water that can neither touch nor be touched. That's the pain of the lower functioning Birthday Sheep. They can only see their own reflection, their own version of "this is me," and therefore they can only love themselves. Yet the only one they love can neither touch nor be touched.

The higher functioning Birthday Sheep, who comprise the majority of Birthday Sheep, have a similar problem, but they have learned how to mask it better. They make less, though still extensive, use of denial, so they learn through interactions with others what they need to do to get the praise they so desperately need. They have learned how to use their socially appropriate relationship skills, but always with a hook. Everything has to be about them, even when others are not aware of what is happening. They get what they need because they feel deserve it.

Another big clue that you are dealing with a Birthday Sheep is name-dropping. The Birthday Sheep will constantly be throwing names of well-known people into the conversation, and always in the context the Birthday Sheep's personal influence on the well-known person. In reality, such influence may be minimal or nonexistent, but not to hear the Birthday Sheep tell it. That is because the real goal in the name-dropping is to impress whoever the Birthday Sheep is talking to, and therefore earn even more praise and admiration for the Birthday Sheep.

Sam was a typical Birthday Sheep. He was a successful insurance salesman, active in Kiwanis, Rotary, and his local congregation. People knew that if you want something done, give it to Sam and he would make it happen. Because he did get things done, and because he was so very easy to like, almost everyone liked Sam.

Most tolerated his stories about his teaching the district manager a way to increase sales, and about his giving ideas to the district governor of Kiwanis that were later implemented with great success. After all, he was a success and he did actually make things happen, so the stories seemed quite believable.

Only those who knew Sam very well did not like him. Like many Birthday Sheep, he had one habit that came out on occasion—he gossiped. He personified the quip "If you can't say something nice about someone, come sit by me."[1] A woman who made the same comments might have been called "catty," but Sam was a man and people who heard his comments liked him enough to not pay much attention. Only the targets of his gossip felt the true venom.

This is another telling characteristic of Birthday Sheep. Their inner world, because it is so empty and so barren, is a world of scarcity. In the deepest reaches of their back stage, they believe the old Western movie cliché: "This town's not big enough for both of us, sheriff." When others receive praise, it is automatically a threat to the Birthday Sheep's sense of self, and therefore the Birthday Sheep feels perfectly righteous in responding to the threat with an attack. It does not matter at all if the other person had no intention of attacking the Birthday Sheep. If someone else receives praise or positive attention, "obviously" there will not be enough left over for the Birthday Sheep. Since praise is the very breath of life for them, to give praise to someone else feels like stealing the oxygen out of the Birthday Sheep's lungs. It is a direct threat to the Birthday Sheep's very existence.

This is why the Birthday Sheep's gossip is so venomous. Those who are so targeted are those who have been found to be a threat to the Birthday Sheep. Of course, most Birthday Sheep are too skilled to be obvious and say things that are actually slanderous. More often, they will be expressed as though they were actually expressions of concern. That way, the Birthday Sheep gets to assassinate the other person and still look good: "Poor, Jane. Did you hear that she got drunk and made a total fool of herself the other night? When I saw what was happening, I said to the mayor, we need to take her home before her husband is even more embarrassed."

Another variation on the same theme is one of the Birthday Sheep's favorite games: "Let's you and him fight." Birthday Sheep are very skilled at diverting all negative attention from themselves because they need the positive attention so much. Thus, when things are not going well, one of the Birthday Sheep's most effective tactics is to go to Jim and tell him what Sarah did, and then go to Sarah and tell her what Jim did. Most often, the Birthday Sheep will make these contacts in a way that makes it seem as though he is sharing special information just with the person he is talking to. Then, when conflict eventually erupts between Jim and Sarah, the Birthday Sheep gets to stand back, above the fray, and appear to have nothing to do with what happened. And because both Jim and Sarah each feel special because they were "warned" by the Birthday Sheep, they will often not even think that the Birthday Sheep had anything to do with what happened. Jim thinks it was all Sarah's fault, and Sarah thinks it was all Jim's fault, and both feel only gratitude to the Birthday Sheep for warning them in advance. This scenario happens all too often in both churches and the workplace. For this reason the shepherd must constantly look beyond the surface when conflict occurs to find the true source.

What is important for the shepherd to remember is that all of this is unconscious for the Birthday Sheep. They are not being deliberately mean or vicious. They are not bad people. The problem is that they genuinely cannot understand how others feel. They can look themselves in the mirror each morning and feel good about themselves because their denial keeps them from seeing their inner emptiness, or the damage they cause when they feel threatened. Like Narcissus in the Greek myth, they see only their own reflection, the superiority they believe they possess, totally unaware of the real world around them.

LEADING THE BIRTHDAY SHEEP

All the major world religions contain an emphasis on placing God and others before one's self. Buddhists say the path to Nirvana is through denial of earthly desires. Muslims say the path to Paradise is through submitting to the will of Allah. Jews say that the will of God is found in loving God with all that is in you and loving others as you do yourself.[2] Since Jesus quoted these parts of the Torah as the summary of the law and the prophets[3] Christians share this belief. So it is natural that when a lower functioning Birthday Sheep comes across as blatantly self-centered, one would be tempted to moralize to him about his selfish ambition and pride. A Christian might say, "Put the clamps on it; beat it down; get humble. There is only one Head in the body of Christ, and it isn't you. If you are famous, don't know it. Be surprised with your success. Become teachable, a servant, and let God lead. It doesn't matter what you think; it's Christ's approval that counts." People from other religious traditions would frame it in terms of their own belief system, but the essential message would be the same.

Of course, the Birthday Sheep is unable to hear such a confrontation without feeling injured, attacked, and enraged. He has to devalue anyone who tries to reach him this way. A more effective means of reaching the Birthday Sheep is to use your empathic understanding to give voice to his real feelings. For example, you might say, "Todd, God understands your needs and your feelings perfectly. He knows how you wish others would understand you and appreciate you, and how when they don't give you the appreciation you believe you deserve, it is almost as though someone has popped your balloon and let all the air out of you. God also understands how sensitive you feel when someone criticizes you, and why it has sometimes been easy for you to devalue and dismiss critical people, because, if you don't, you feel so injured, small, and worthless." This example shows why the shepherd who is working with a Birthday Sheep needs a tremendous ability to self-soothe.

To be quite honest, there may be times when all the shepherd feels like doing is throttling the Birthday Sheep or shaking some sense into him. The opportunity for real ministry with the Birthday Sheep will likely come, however, only when he is already emotionally unstable, possibly even attacking the shepherd. Giving voice to the Birthday Sheep's feelings, without being judgmental or critical, allows the Birthday Sheep to see the shepherd as a friend and ally. While it certainly will not fill the emptiness at the center of the Birthday Sheep's life, it can at least head off a potential interpersonal explosion in the church.

Higher functioning Birthday Sheep like Sam do make good church leaders—as long as they are working in solo positions. If the shepherd will use the normal leadership skills of selecting people based on their talents, and if the shepherd will make a point of giving appropriate praise, the Birthday Sheep should do quite well. Be warned, though: Birthday Sheep make poor committee leaders. They will tend to grab all the attention for themselves, which can be frustrating for other committee members, even the most self-secure Wednesday Sheep. And if others should happen to commit the "sin" of being better than the Birthday Sheep, the Birthday Sheep will feel injured and thus will find ways to undercut, damage, or devalue the offending committee member. Often, this will be through the "Let's you and him fight" game, or through using the venomous gossip at which the Birthday Sheep is so skilled. Either way, the Birthday Sheep is able to look good to others, which is the main point of these tactics. The end result, however, is dissention, hurt feelings, and greater division for the church.

Another means of leading the Birthday Sheep is to preach sermons and present Bible studies that focus on God's unconditional acceptance of us. These sermons can give voice to the Birthday Sheep's deep desire to be loved and accepted, while not making that acceptance contingent on anything the Birthday Sheep does. However it is phrased, the message should be similar to that of twentieth-century theologian Paul Tillich, who often emphasized, "Simply accept the fact that you are accepted."[4]

This is often easier said than done. Because the Birthday Sheep's conscious sense of entitlement is so strong, they will usually go to the senior pastor rather than the associate pastor or the youth director or whoever is supposed to be in charge. This can also cause conflict because the person whom the Birthday Sheep should have gone to might perceive this as "going over their head," which stirs feelings of resentment. This is just as common in the workplace as in a church setting. Since the Birthday Sheep, especially a lower functioning one, will resist or resent any efforts to send him back to the "underling," the best the secure shepherd in such a situation can do is listen and then carefully brief the person who is in charge so that no one is caught in the middle of a game of "let's you and him fight."

Similarly, if there is only one minister in charge, the Birthday Sheep may go to the denominational official (for example, the association minister or the district superintendent) with complaints of "long overdue" expressions of appreciation. It is hard to be the shepherd in charge and not feel undermined or extremely frustrated by such actions. Ministry in this context, however, means recognizing that the Birthday Sheep is merely acting on his inner sense of entitlement, and that it has little, if anything, to do with what the shepherd may have done wrong. Good, accurate self-talk is the best way of keeping one's self from being as emotionally reactive as the Birthday Sheep is. We would recommend every shepherd have a small support group so that when a Birthday Sheep (or any type of sheep) begins to get under his or her skin the shepherd will have someone to talk things out with and who will help put the situation in the proper perspective. Even the best functioning, wisest leader can quickly lose perspective when being attacked or feeling as if he or she is being undermined.

If you are a shepherd doing premarital counseling, a clue that one partner is a Birthday Sheep is that the other partner is so totally wrapped up in the Birthday Sheep. Birthday Sheep tend to attract those who are dependent, or codependent. Their aura of self-confidence is highly attractive to those who feel inadequate and want to be protected. If you observe a relationship that seems to be unusually intense and one-way, you could well be working with a dependent–Birthday Sheep couple.

Naturally, this does not bode well for the future of the marriage. Eventually, the dependent partner will not be able to keep up with the levels of admiration that the Birthday Sheep needs. When that happens, the Birthday Sheep will feel devalued and attacked, responding in rage by devaluing and attacking in return. Naturally, the dependent person will not have any idea what prompted the attacks and so may pull back in puzzled self-protection. Of course, the Birthday Sheep will feel the pulling back as further evidence of an attack, and so the cycle will repeat. The couple may not divorce. The Birthday Sheep will not want a divorce because that would be incontrovertible evidence that he is less than perfect. And the dependent or codependent partner may not feel she could survive if she did divorce. Whether they divorce or not, the future of the relationship likely will be like two porcupines trying to share body heat in a burrow on a cold night. They can only get just so close without one or the other feeling pricked. Cold drives them together and pain drives them apart. That is the dance of relationship in a Birthday Sheep's marriage.

Marital counseling with a Birthday Sheep is beyond the scope of any local church pastor. There will be more on counseling Birthday Sheep later in this chapter. During premarital counseling, the shepherd can work with the more dependent partner to help her gain a sense of self. Basic relationship skills, such as being appropriately assertive and being able to use the listening skills described in this book, can help. Some good self-talk so that the Birthday Sheep can begin to self-soothe and not be so totally focused on his partner's affirmation will also be helpful. Still, this is a deeply ingrained pattern that will not change easily. The best one can hope for is to help the couple limit the amount of inevitable damage they will both feel.

THE BIRTHDAY SHEEP AS SHEPHERD

In 2003, Wayne published the results of his research on clergy candidates in the *Journal for Pastoral Care*.[5] After looking at more than fifty clergy candidates from one particular denomination, he found that clergy candidates had a significantly greater need for others' affirmation than the average person. In fact, the clergy candidates in this sample had a higher need for others' affirmation than ninety-five out of one hundred people in the general population. Wayne's more than thirty years of experience as a pastor and as a therapist supports his impression that this finding was not a fluke or confined to any one denomination. Birthday Sheep are particularly attracted to a profession like ministry.

Why this is so seems to be fairly easy to understand. At least within the Christian denominations with which we are most familiar, almost inevitably when someone comes forward claiming to be called by God into ministry that person receives a great deal of praise and support from others in the congregation. The Birthday Sheep often has a rather winsome personality, and the Birthday Sheep's aura of self-confidence makes it seem as though this person is particularly suited for positions of leadership. So all during the candidacy process, whatever that may look like in a given denomination, the Birthday Sheep is highly likely to find the praise and affirmation he has longed for all his life. The Birthday Sheep will see the preacher standing in front of the congregation each week and notice how all the people come to hear the word from God that he brings. "Oh, how I would love to have all those people hanging on my every word," he may think on his back stage. Further, the biblical messages of God's love and acceptance are strongly attractive to the Birthday Sheep. So candidacy for ministry is almost custom made for the emotional needs of a Birthday Sheep.

Before we go on, we want to explicitly say that nothing in these comments is intended to cast doubt on the reality of God's call to certain people, even those who might seem to be damaged in some way. God called Moses despite his stuttering, Saul despite his lack of self-confidence, Jeremiah despite his tendency toward depression.[6] God can call even deeply wounded people like Birthday Sheep, and our personal belief system says God can effectively use these people. We will leave it to various denominational leaders to determine who is genuinely called by God and who may be responding to his or her own inner needs.

Whatever the case, when the Birthday Sheep becomes a shepherd, sooner or later the rough and tumble of congregational life is bound to take its toll. While the Birthday Sheep will likely do well in short-term pastorates, in longer assignments sooner or later some leader will emerge within the congregation who will attract more favorable comments than the Birthday Sheep Shepherd. If that person happens to be an associate pastor or another member of the church staff, the Birthday Sheep Shepherd will almost surely set up a "Let's you and him fight" with one or more members of the congregation. Many young clergy have had their ministries ruined and lost the joy of their service due to just such an encounter with a threatened Birthday Sheep senior pastor, and they may never know what really happened.

The Birthday Sheep shepherd's relationships with other clergy will be similarly problematic. The Birthday Sheep shepherd will make sure all his colleagues, especially those in positions of power and influence within the denomination, will know of all his accomplishments. He is a great "spin doctor," putting a positive spin on everything so that even the most modest accomplishments will appear to be great. Other clergy may feel jealous of the attention the Birthday Sheep tries to grab. Of course, if they should be so brash as to do something right that attracts attention, the Birthday Sheep Shepherd will likely use gossip among colleagues to poison and devalue the accomplishments of his "rivals." No wonder so many studies report that clergy do not trust their fellow clergy. While by no means are all clergy Birthday Sheep, there are enough in the profession, and they are hard enough to spot (very few of the lower functioning Birthday Sheep make it into ministry; they usually get spotted and eliminated during whatever candidacy process there may be) that one never knows who among one's colleagues to trust.

WHEN BIRTHDAY SHEEP NEED HELP

Perhaps, by now, the psychologically astute reader will have surmised that Birthday Sheep represent the relatively normal expression of what mental health professionals call Narcissistic Personality Disorder (NPD). According to the American Psychiatric Association, less than 1 percent of the general population will meet the criteria for this disorder. Of those who do, however, 50 to 75 percent will be male[7] (which, not so coincidentally, is the same male-female ratio as Birthday Sheep). Birthday Sheep will share most of the characteristics as someone with NPD, just not with a severe enough expression to warrant the mental health diagnosis.

Even among those who do warrant the diagnosis, few are willing to volunteer for treatment. The reason why is quite simple. Unlike Monday or Tuesday Sheep, Birthday Sheep (like those with the full NPD) do not find their way of living painful or uncomfortable. To them, it is perfectly normal. They may well cause others pain, but their lack of (or greatly decreased) empathy keeps them from realizing what they are doing. If others are uncomfortable or unhappy, well, that is their problem, according to the Birthday Sheep. If a Birthday Sheep does come for counseling, most probably it will be for help "fixing" someone else, like a spouse. Pastors, and even counselors, need to be very careful in such situations. What may happen is that they may inadvertently teach the Birthday Sheep how to become an even more skillful manipulator of relationships.

If the Birthday Sheep truly does want to change, the therapy will definitely be long term. Therapists skilled in a cognitive therapy, such as Cognitive-Behavioral and/or Adlerian, can help the Birthday Sheep enter the void that permeates their back stage and start to construct a genuine sense of self. Personality change is possible, but it is tedious, often painful work, like pulling layers of adhesive tape off of a very hairy leg—only longer and much more painful. Someone would have to be very powerfully motivated to endure to the end. This is most definitely not the kind of work any pastor, or even most therapists, would have the time, the training, or the temperament to undertake. Like teens, Birthday Sheep are very volatile and very manipulative, but unlike teens, they are usually much more skillful, and more covert, in their manipulation. It is a rare therapist who can withstand the attacks and manipulation of the Birthday Sheep without giving even subtle hints at rejection.

Most shepherds are best served by recognizing Birthday Sheep in their fold and taking steps to allow them opportunities to express their gifts so that the Birthday Sheep can receive the praise they so desperately crave. At the same time, the shepherd will need to take steps to minimize the interpersonal damage a Birthday Sheep is likely to cause. If the shepherd can accomplish these twin tasks, that will be real leadership indeed.

Living into the Lesson

1. How do you respond when you encounter persons who think the world should revolve around them? Are you able to lead them or do they cause you frustration?
2. How intentional are you at spreading praise among your flock? How do you respond to the person who seeks/demands that praise?

3. How intentional are you at leading teenagers? Do teens frustrate or excite you? What strategies have you found that work with teenagers also work with Birthday Sheep?
4. How would you have responded to Sam?
5. When have you been pulled into the game of "let's you and him fight"? What circumstances led you into being caught in that game? How have you avoided it?
6. How do you respond when you feel criticized or attacked? Are you able to look past the attack and respond to the person? What would help you be more effective in your response?
7. How do you respond when someone "goes over your head"? Do you attack, circle the wagons, or try to reach out to the person? Think of a time when you've responded well and a time when you didn't handle it so well. What lessons did you learn?
8. Why do you think ministry would be an attractive profession for Birthday Sheep? What potential problems do you see?

7

SATURDAY SHEEP

I'm one of those regular weird people.

—JANICE JOPLIN, AMERICAN SINGER

Saturday is, of course, the last day of the week. It is appropriate, then, the final examination of the sheep within your flock will focus on Saturday Sheep. Before we begin our look at who Saturday Sheep are and how one can best lead them, a word of disclaimer is in order. Many people honor Saturday as their Sabbath. For these people, Saturday Sheep should be called Sunday Sheep—the other day of the weekend. With that small editorial change, all the other observations will still apply. It's not the day that really matters but the principle.

For most Americans, Saturday is the first day of the weekend. It is a day for going to the lake, working in the garden, watching football, or whatever else constitutes "fun." All week long, we

Americans are driven and responsible. On Saturday, however, we get to put responsibilities aside and just play. Sunday will be a day of worship for many Christians, and Monday will be another workday, but Saturday is a day to shun obligation and simply do what I want to do. For Saturday Sheep, every day is like that. Every day is a Saturday.

CHARACTERISTICS OF THE SATURDAY SHEEP

Saturday Sheep represent only a small minority of the flock, yet they will demand extraordinary amounts of the shepherd's time. Frequently, this can be positive attention, and it can be quite flattering for the shepherd. After all, who does not enjoy positive attention? Indeed, the Saturday Sheep may often go out of her way to tell the preacher what a wonderful sermon he just preached, and how his routine visit to her home made such a tremendous difference in her life. Accustomed, as most clergy are, to being more or less taken for granted, this can be heady stuff indeed.

We use "her" in this case because about 75 percent of Saturday Sheep are female. They can be almost any age, from teen all the way through old age. While there are various theories as to what causes someone to become a Saturday Sheep, no clear consensus has been reached and no research has been to done to adequately explain why such a huge percentage are female. Until modern science comes up with some answers, prevention is going to be largely out of the question. So, proper leadership of those who are Saturday Sheep is currently the best solution.

Our previous statement about "prevention" might cause one to wonder why anyone would want to prevent compliments. The answer is, the compliments are only part of the Saturday Sheep's story. Unlike Birthday Sheep, Saturday Sheep can genuinely care about others and can give to others. That is the attractive side. Like the Birthday Sheep, however, their caring always comes with a hook. Saturday Sheep give to, and care for, others because they expect to be cared for in return. In fact, the intensity of their positive attention is a measure of the negative attention they can display if they do not receive "enough" care in return.

To see why this is such a danger, let us return once more to the hypothetical sermon in which you are addressing the believer's responsibility to help others, to be active in the church, and to give financially—the sermon the Monday and Tuesday Sheep heard as all law and obligation, and the Birthday Sheep heard as evidence of his spiritual superiority. What does the Saturday Sheep hear? At least in the early stages of her relationship with the preacher, she will probably consider this an excellent sermon, regardless of what the preacher's homiletics professor might have thought. "Yes, he cares so deeply for our church. What words of wisdom he is bringing us! It's like the voice of God is speaking right to us!" She may even tell the preacher her thoughts as she is leaving the church, and then drop by again on Monday morning to tell him one more time, in even more detail, how wonderful the sermon was.

At first the preacher will no doubt appreciate these intrusions into his day and make time for them. Even when, or perhaps especially when, the preacher is personally convinced that the sermon was far from his best, having a member of the congregation express such appreciation for his efforts, however flawed, feels good. And the Saturday Sheep likely will not confine her compliments to just the sermon. Every Bible study, every committee meeting, in fact every act of ministry will be a spiritual gem that she must take time to compliment.

Eventually, all of this will be too much—unless, of course, the shepherd happens to be a Birthday Sheep. In that case, the Saturday Sheep will simply be giving the Birthday Sheep what the Birthday Sheep believes he so richly deserves and what so few other people recognize. In a twisted sort of way, it is a match made in heaven, at least at first. Most often, however, the Saturday Sheep will catch the shepherd at an inopportune moment. Perhaps he has to prepare for a particularly difficult committee meeting, or perhaps he has just come from the funeral of a member of the congregation to whom he was particularly close. Whatever the reason, sooner or later the pastor will not be as emotionally available as the Saturday Sheep believes he "ought" to be. This will be the start of a downhill slide in the relationship, a slide from which there likely will be no turning back.

Alice is a typical Saturday Sheep. When Brother Paul became the pastor of the congregation of which she was a member, she was among the first to welcome him and his family. She organized the church's official welcome reception, and she made a point of telling the elders how pleased she was that Brother Paul had been called to that church. Whenever anyone would make even a slightly negative comment about Brother Paul, Alice was his strongest cheerleader and supporter. None of this was lost on Brother Paul. He and his wife frequently told Alice how much they appreciated her and her support.

The honeymoon lasted for nearly a year. Eventually, however, Brother Paul tired of Alice dropping by—sometimes with an appointment, sometimes not—to talk with him about an assortment of different issues. At times Alice wanted to compliment Brother Paul about something she thought he had done "right," while at other times she wanted his guidance on how she should deal with various issues, such as dealing with her children, her husband, and conflicts with church members, to name only a few. It seemed Paul could get little else done but talk with Alice. Paul found he was not as willing to delay his planned hospital visits as he had been just because Alice happened to drop by. He began to gently urge Alice along when she was overflowing with compliments after Sunday sermons. Alice noticed the difference but kept on giving for a while. After all, she did genuinely like Brother Paul. One Wednesday afternoon the final slight came. Paul had agreed to meet with Alice over her concerns about her daughter but his meeting with the chair of his finance committee ran about ten minutes longer than he anticipated. For Alice, his being late was the final straw. It was evidence that he was a mean, cruel, heartless man who had no business even attending a church, much less leading one.

From that point forward, Alice never missed an opportunity to tell all her friends what an evil man Paul was. She quit attending the church and made a point of calling all her friends who still attended the church to tell them she thought they were mistaken to listen to such an "evil" influence. While Paul managed to survive as pastor there for several more years and did eventually move on to another, larger congregation, Alice had taken her toll. Paul's remaining years of ministry at that congregation were marked by his constantly having to defend himself. Because he was in a "defensive crouch," little constructive happened those last years. The congregation just marked time.

Paul's experience with Alice is typical of the relationships Saturday Sheep have, and this includes with their spouse. In the early days, their relationship is marked by idealization of the other person—this person can do no wrong. Since this is the world after the fall, however, sooner or later the other must eventually disappoint the Saturday Sheep one too many times. When that invisible line is crossed—and there is no way to know where that line is, much less how to avoid crossing it—the other person becomes a spawn of Satan, the personification of evil, as far as the Saturday Sheep is concerned. This switch from the personification of good to the personification of evil can happen with such rapidity that the target almost feels like he or she has whiplash. And at lower levels of functioning, this switch can go back and forth repeatedly, which keeps the other person constantly insecure as to where the relationship is going to be at any given moment. Being in a relationship with a lower functioning Saturday Sheep is, to use an old Southern expression, like being a long-tailed cat in a room full of rocking chairs.

Many shepherds will have experienced this phenomenon without knowing it. Think back to a person whom you grew steadily weary of being around—who used up inordinate amounts of your time. This same person might begin as your friend, but over time you begin to dread every time your phone rings or you hear someone coming into your office because you're afraid it might be that individual. Your entire life becomes more stressful because of this one person.

This is a big hint that you are dealing with a Saturday Sheep—the shepherd will hear stories of chaotic relationships surrounding the Saturday Sheep from multiple sources, stories that involve multiple settings. The alert shepherd will listen for these stories, because they may well give a warning of trouble to come before the shepherd actually becomes the target.

Another clue will be the Saturday Sheep's tendency toward substance abuse. She may abuse alcohol or prescription drugs. Likely, she will hide this well, so there may not be any overt signs. In other words, the Saturday Sheep may not show up for worship smelling of alcohol or obviously high on prescription painkillers. But if the shepherd should hear concerns from a spouse or children about substance abuse that is being well hidden, those stories could be true and a telling sign that the substance abusing spouse is a Saturday Sheep. Similarly, stories about substance abuse among the children, especially preteen children, could point to the presence of a Saturday Sheep. Not every teen who experiments with drugs is the child of a Saturday Sheep, but those who live with one or more Saturday Sheep find the experience unsettling and painful. They may find that turning to drugs is the easiest way to deal with their inner pain.

Saturday Sheep may marry almost any other kind of sheep. Should two Saturday Sheep marry, the result will inevitably be an exceptionally chaotic relationship. The two partners will be tightly bound together, sometimes madly in love with each other, and other times slashing and cutting each other, verbally if not physically. Police may well have been called to the house on more than one occasion. An image of this relationship is the story told about the old Apache warriors. Allegedly, when two warriors could not settle their disagreements, they were bound together by their left wrists, and each was given a knife to hold in his right hand. They then could slash at each other, unable to run away, until one of them was dead. We cannot verify whether the Apache warriors ever actually engaged in this ritual or not, but it's a perfect picture of two Saturday Sheep in a relationship. They are bound together by their fear of abandonment, yet their relationship style cuts and wounds the one to whom they are most tightly bound.

A Saturday Sheep may marry a Birthday Sheep, and for a while this can be a wonderfully intense relationship. Eventually, however, the Birthday Sheep's inability to give back will be tiring for the Saturday Sheep, and then the fireworks will start. Of course, the Birthday Sheep will respond to these attacks with attacks of his own, and the end result can be as chaotic as the relationship of two Saturday Sheep.

A Saturday Sheep may marry either a Monday or a Tuesday Sheep as a "do-it-yourself" project. She loves and wants to be loved, and she believes that if she can just "fix" them, they will love her. She is wrong. The Monday Sheep is too anxious and the Tuesday Sheep too pessimistic to love the Saturday Sheep "enough." Sooner or later, these relationships, too, will descend into chaos.

Finally, Saturday Sheep may marry Wednesday Sheep. The Wednesday Sheep will accurately experience the Saturday Sheep's love and may find the attention gratifying. The 1987 movie *Fatal Attraction* graphically illustrates an extreme of what the outcome might be. While the movie does focus on an affair, not a marriage, and while it is more than a bit overdone, the portrayal by Glenn Close as Alex Forrest is masterfully similar to what a Saturday Sheep matched with a Wednesday Sheep might act like. Dan

Gallagher (Michael Douglas) is a happily married man who is attracted by Alex's flirtatious self-confidence. What he believes will be simply a one-night stand while his wife is out of town becomes a living nightmare. The Wednesday Sheep who marries a Saturday Sheep will similarly find the relationship wonderful at first, but eventually it will become a nightmare for both of them.

Close's performance in *Fatal Attraction* vividly illustrates another hint that the shepherd is dealing with a Saturday Sheep—self-destruction. In the movie, Alex Forrest was a lawyer, an intelligent and successful woman in her own right. But in her drive to keep the relationship with Dan going, she threw it all away. Her behavior spun increasingly out of control until it finally ended in tragedy.

Most Saturday Sheep do not go to the lengths of Alex Forrest, but their behavior is still self-destructive. They may engage in excessive spending or gambling. They may, like Alex, engage in numerous adulterous affairs. They may drive recklessly and/or drunk. The possibilities are almost limitless. One thing the shepherd should remember is that "self-destructive" does not necessarily mean suicidal. Only in very rare cases does the Saturday Sheep intend to die. Indeed, the Tuesday Sheep is far more likely to commit suicide than the Saturday Sheep. The Saturday Sheep's self-destructive behavior is actually aimed at trying to feel alive. Like the Birthday Sheep, their inner core is empty. Unlike the Birthday Sheep, they know it is empty, so they try to fill the emptiness with thrilling experiences. If they are adjusted enough, or care enough about society norms, they may not engage in self-destructive behavior through alcohol or drug addiction, but may, instead, become addicted to adrenaline rushes such as sky diving, bungee jumping, or anything else that creates a "rush." Regardless of the method us, trying to fill this void is a bit like trying to fill the Grand Canyon with a teaspoon, and the resulting painful recognition of the futility is what fuels the Saturday Sheep's tendency toward substance abuse.

LEADING THE SATURDAY SHEEP

Unlike the Monday or Tuesday Sheep, for whom life is only gray, Saturday Sheep believe that life should be happy. They usually wish to cling to someone who will take care of them and make them feel good. Correspondingly, they may even relate in these ways to God. They may especially like the idea of "let go and let God," interpreting this saying to mean that God will relieve them of some particular normal adult responsibility while they remain passive, inert, and helpless. If God would just do that, then the Christian life would be simple, easy, and managed for them. God truly would make every day a Saturday for them. For example, they may expect God to remove all pain and suffering in their own life or in the lives of those they love, and do so instantly. When this unrealistic expectation is not fulfilled, they may feel disappointed with God and then afraid God may abandon them for feeling disappointed. It is a "catch-22" that is so typical of Saturday Sheep. They feel disappointed but cannot voice their disappointment (and thus potentially resolve or reduce it) for fear of being abandoned.

Saturday Sheep also tend to emphasize love in their religious language. Now, obviously, this resonates with most, if not all, other religious people, but few realize that the Saturday Sheep defines "love" in a unique way. For the Saturday Sheep, love equals need. The person who is needy, inadequate, and/or unable to be an independently functioning person is lovable. The person who is not needy is not loveable. If they can find someone who needs them, a person to whom they can minister, they feel confident that they will not be abandoned, which is their one greatest fear in life. They can love only those who need them and they truly need to be needed. They truly and deeply believe that line from the 1996 movie *Jerry McGuire*: "You complete me." Unless they are needed, they are incomplete and therefore unlovable and thus very likely to be abandoned.

Now, unlike the Birthday Sheep, the Saturday Sheep is keenly aware of her neediness, and therefore she should be very loveable to God and to others. This is why she expects the shepherd, as God's representative, to act lovingly toward her. Like Alex Forrest, she may be very seductive and sexually aggressive. Seducing the shepherd is almost as good as seducing God and practically guarantees her permanent acceptance, at least in her mind. Therefore, shepherds who are not appropriately getting their emotional needs met are very vulnerable to crossing the many boundaries into perpetrating clergy sexual abuse. The fact that the Saturday Sheep may have initiated the contact is no excuse, nor does it make it not abuse. The shepherd is the one with the "power," and any inappropriate contact, regardless of who initiates it, is abuse of that power by the shepherd. This is why so many denominations are, thankfully, taking a strong stand on clergy sexual ethics. But what if the shepherd does not respond to all the Saturday Sheep's neediness, as Dan failed to respond to Alex in *Fatal Attraction*? It is again evidence to the Saturday Sheep that she is as unlovable as she has feared in the deepest recesses of her back stage. Should the shepherd preach sermons that emphasize the holiness of God, the "otherness" of God that is above human need, that act will be felt as very threatening for the Saturday Sheep. Conversely, sermons that talk about God's love and how God responds to humankind will bring joy to the Saturday Sheep's soul.

One positive, preventative note a wise shepherd can sound from time to time is, in the words of Saint Paul, "Therefore, my beloved, just as you have always obeyed me, not only in my presence, but much more now in my absence, work out your own salvation with fear and trembling; for it is God who is at work in you, enabling you both to will and to work for his good pleasure" (Phil. 2:12–13). Anyone who has studied the writings of Paul knows that he is not talking about salvation by works. His discussions of salvation by grace through faith make that abundantly clear. Rather, here he is talking about the process of working out in every area of your life what it means to have been saved by God's grace. In other words, if you have faith that you are involved in the process of salvation, God expects you to activate yourself 100 percent in this process. Readers from traditions other than the Christian tradition may have to translate this into terms of their own faith heritage, but the note will be similar. God does not expect us to merely relax and let God do all the work. At a very minimum, we are to be cocreators with God in building God's realm. The Saturday Sheep needs to hear that, along with assurance of pardon. Saturday Sheep live with a very deep sense of shame, of being uniquely flawed. Hearing repeatedly of a loving, forgiving, accepting God who also expects our best efforts and pardons our failings can help the Saturday Sheep find at last a stable point on which to hang her spiritual life.

Saturday Sheep make very poor leaders in the church. They may very much want to be involved, and they may (as Alex Forrest showed) be genuinely talented people. Unfortunately, their style of relationships is even more unstable than the Birthday Sheep, so their talent often gets tainted by their volatility. Even so, if they are placed in highly structured situations where "success" and "need" are very clear cut, they can function well enough and indeed achieve real success. Saturday Sheep are generally not good entrepreneurs who function well in chaotic or unstructured environments. The wise shepherd will give them short-term, clearly defined situations, and within those situations Saturday Sheep can very well excel. For example, they might do fine in a disaster relief situation where they clean up homes damaged by a storm, or where they pass out food to victims of a storm. Such situations are usually short-term enough that the objects of their ministry (notice that phrase) do not have time to appear "ungrateful" and therefore abandoning and therefore threatening.

THE SATURDAY SHEEP AS SHEPHERD

In our research for this book, we could find no evidence of a Saturday Sheep as a shepherd, and in our own personal experience, we cannot say that we have ever met a minister we believed to be a Saturday Sheep. It may very well have happened at some point, but we were unable to find documented cases where it has.

To us, this makes perfect sense. Saturday Sheep are too unstable in their relationships. Their tendency toward impulsive, self-destructive behavior is too likely to catch unfavorable attention. Based on the lack of references to them in the literature, we would have to say that probably most Saturday Sheep who try to enter professional ministry are eliminated at some point during the process of candidacy. This is not to say that Saturday Sheep may not be attracted to ministry for many of the same reasons as a Birthday Sheep. They can indeed love others far more genuinely than Birthday Sheep, and they do need to be needed. The chance to have others needing the connecting to God that they can bring through their sermons, their visits, their wisdom . . . that need to be needed would be a powerful attractant for the Saturday Sheep. As true as that is, ministry is essentially relational in ways that few, if any, other professions are. One can have a quirky personality and still be a very competent lawyer, physician, or accountant. Few people would accept these same quirks in their religious leader. For that reason, we believe, there are few if any Saturday Sheep who last long in professional ministry, even if they make it through the initial denominational screening process.

WHEN SATURDAY SHEEP NEED HELP

Saturday Sheep represent the more "normal" functioning range of what psychotherapists call Borderline Personality Disorder (BPD). According to data published by the American Psychiatric Association in the DSM-IV,[1] about 2 percent of the U.S. population meet the criteria for BPD. Other studies, however, suggest that between 30 and 60 percent of people who are actually in therapy have BPD or BPD "features" (that is, they are Saturday Sheep). Furthermore, again according to the American Psychiatric Association, BPD is five times more likely among first-degree biological relatives.[2]

For those of you not used to psychological terms, that information can seem a little overwhelming, but these facts can help the wise shepherd draw two conclusions. First, while the Saturday Sheep will be a very small minority in their flock, they will be inordinately present in the shepherd's counseling load, as well as most other areas of the shepherd's life. Since most licensed therapists will seldom accept more than one patient at a time with BPD because these clients are so demanding and so emotionally draining, the pastor should be very careful about scanning the people in his or her counseling load. As the case with Alice illustrates, working with these clients can be an emotional high at first, but the eventual cost can far outweigh the few original benefits. Keeping all pastoral counseling brief, short-term, and solution-focused will keep the pastor from getting trapped by the neediness (read that as "lovability" in the Saturday Sheep's language) of the Saturday Sheep. As a rule of thumb no pastor, no matter how well trained, should see a member of the congregation more than three times. If the situation cannot be resolved in that short time, a referral to a competent mental health professional is essential for both the pastor's health and the congregation member's. Following this rule enables the pastor to make the referral without seeming to the Saturday Sheep as rejecting or abandoning the Saturday Sheep. It is just the way this shepherd cares for all his flock.

The second conclusion from the American Psychiatric Association's facts is that if you have one Saturday Sheep in a family, you are very likely to have other Saturday Sheep in that same family. If the Saturday Sheep in your congregation has no other family members in your congregation, this fact might be of only academic interest. If, however, you have several generations and/or branches of a Saturday Sheep's family in your congregation, it is statistically probable that you will have several Saturday Sheep to deal with. The demands on your time and energy can easily exceed even the most energetic shepherd's efforts, which, as the case with Alice illustrates, inevitably generate multiple sources of attack on the shepherd.

This fact suggests that every pastor should have access to well-trained, religiously sensitive family therapists. While these families are very unlikely to seek treatment for the BPD, they may well be open to treatment for some of the chaos they experience. Family therapists understand that some systems (families, churches, businesses) use chaos to organize themselves, and they also know how to work with these chaotically fused families. This is a work for specialists, not for the busy pastor. Further, the family therapist can give the pastor helpful guidance in providing ministry for all families, not just the chaotic families of Saturday Sheep. We have been speaking of this rule for pastors, but knowing how to find appropriate mental and spiritual help is an essential tool for the toolbox of any leader. Remember from our initial overview that the shepherd's job is to feed, lead, and protect the sheep. The best leadership is knowing when someone else can better tend to that sheep's needs.

In the event that a Saturday Sheep should want to put an end to the shame and emptiness inside, the therapy is best left to someone who has the time and energy to deal with a personality disorder. As previously indicated for the Birthday Sheep, this is long-term work, and it will inevitably be very painful for the Saturday Sheep. It is the province of well-trained, licensed therapists, therapists who understand both personality disorders and family functioning.

Meanwhile, the wise shepherd can make sure the Saturday Sheep do not feel spiritually abandoned by providing the acts of ministry already listed. Working in concert with a properly trained, religiously sensitive therapist, the shepherd can give the Saturday

Sheep what they most want—an assurance they will never be lost or abandoned. They truly can be healed.

Living into the Lesson

1. How do you respond to those who tend to shirk responsibility?
2. How do you respond when someone consistently compliments you? Does this type of attitude stroke your ego or annoy you?
3. Do you have adequate boundaries set up to prevent misconduct when loneliness or stress set in and someone pays you an inordinate amount of positive attention?
4. When have you experienced the "hook" of Saturday Sheep, that is, things went great until you failed in one instance, causing them to turn on you? How did you respond to the situation? What did you learn from this experience?
5. How would you have dealt with Alice? What would you have done when Alice started undercutting your leadership effectiveness?
6. What might you do to help a Saturday Sheep who feels he or she is not loved unless "needed"?
7. What would you do to convey God's acceptance and pardon to someone as needy as a Saturday Sheep?
8. Have you ever had a Saturday Sheep in a place of leadership in your flock? How did that situation turn out? What lessons did you learn?
9. What boundaries have you set on the number of sessions you will counsel a member of your flock? What are your thoughts on the recommendation that you not see any member of your flock more than three times?

8

SHEEP LEADING SHEEP

The guy who puts the ball through the hoop has ten hands.

—JOHN WOODEN, HALL-OF-FAME BASKETBALL COACH

A wise pastor told Wayne when he was very young in the profession, and he passed it on to Chris, "Shepherds don't beget sheep. Sheep beget sheep." A key principle of effective leadership is that the sheep determine what actually happens. This is true whether we are speaking of a church, a business, the military, or any other situation where there are leaders and followers. The shepherd, as the leader of the flock, has very real influence. Still, when it comes to the flock replicating and continuing itself, sheep, not shepherds, beget sheep.

Many leaders, especially in pastoral ministry, have heard that "20 percent of the people do 80 percent of the work." The saying may or may not be objectively true, but it is a good principle.

Carefully choose your Wednesday Sheep as leaders for the flock. Nurture those Wednesday Sheep. Spend time with them so that they catch the shepherd's vision and make it their own. Once they truly own the shepherd's vision, they will "beget" other sheep who also share this vision.

As we previously discussed, however, most people are Wednesday Sheep—that is, they are mostly emotionally and spiritually healthy and functioning well. How does the shepherd know which ones to select as leaders? By listening between the lines, as we have outlined in this book. That is not always an easy task, but we hope to have provided you with some tools to make the job a little easier. Watch to whom people actually speak. Listen to the stories—who has actually wielded power to make things happen in the past? In other words, who already has relational authority, regardless of having positional authority? Observe these people in their interactions—do they give evidence of being open systems or closed systems? Often, the people with the real power in the congregation may have very little positional power. To use a cliché, it does not matter who sits on the throne. What matters is the person with power behind the throne. One of the biggest mistakes a young shepherd can make is to assume the one with the title has the power.

While these real leaders may or may not be a literal 20 percent of the congregation, they will be relatively few in number, and the shepherd should devote the majority of his or her time to these leaders. Listen carefully to them. Take what they say seriously—the front stage and the back stage rules. Jointly work out a way that they can manage their own anxiety, and the anxiety of the other sheep, while the congregation is in flux moving from one homeostasis to another. Allow them to help you choose sheep-leaders to assist with special projects or ministries, and encourage them to help you know how to best shepherd these other sheep for their leadership positions.

We have read countless books on leadership, and most of them espouse similar recommendations. Then why are they so seldom followed? Shepherds, as much as sheep, are subject to back stage rules. For instance, seminary training tends to focus on the pastor as *the* leader, the prima dona (a ballet term denoting "primary dancer"). Most of the models of ministry lived out in congregations over the last thirty years have been, from our observation, pastor-centered. All responsibility for vision, training, leadership, ministry, and administration is centered on the senior pastor. The senior pastor has truly become a CEO-type figure.

Well, what is wrong with that? After all, the pastor is the leader of the flock. Should he or she not know where God is trying to lead the flock? We would never want to question the pastor's obligation to faithfully proclaim the vision the pastor has received from God. There is ample biblical evidence that this is an essential part of the pastor/shepherd's job description. To do so from a pastor-centered position, however, rather than by listening to the sheep and sending sheep to beget sheep, has a very real consequence for leadership.

In literal sheep farming, some flocks have a very clear leader. The shepherd may put a bell on that particular sheep. With or without the bell, the other sheep readily follow that leader sheep. All the shepherd has to do is guide that one sheep to good food and water, and watch out for outside dangers. The rest of the flock readily follows along. Other flocks, however, have no clear leader. In these flocks, a good sheep dog is an absolute necessity. Because they have no clear leader, sheep are constantly wandering off in one direction or another. The sheep dog is continually running from one sheep to another to try to keep the flock together. The moments of rest are few and far between for the sheep dog, and even these demand vigilance, not relaxation. Sooner than later, another sheep will wander off, and it's time to dash again.

Shepherds who do not train up leaders in the flock will live their ministry more like a sheep dog than a shepherd. They may be able to herd the entire flock in a desired direction, but it will be accomplished through mad dashing first after this crisis, then after that one. They are constantly in a reactive mode, so despite their frantic activity and illusions of being in charge, they are really just reacting to the competing agendas set by the wandering sheep. No wonder so many pastors burn out and leave ministry. Even those burned-out pastors who continue to fill pulpits show their burnout by becoming more involved in the denomination's politics than in the local congregation's spiritual life, or by getting involved in pornography, illicit affairs, substance abuse problems, or a host of other attempts to numb their underlying anxiety about never being able to do it "right." Shepherds were never meant to be sheep dogs, and those who try will inevitably pay a price.

If this were a perfect world, all the pastor/shepherd would need to do would be to listen between the lines to accurately discern the true needs of the sheep, and then recruit and train sheep leaders to meet those needs. Remember that one of those key needs is the need for constant improvement spiritually, as well as mentally and emotionally. To borrow a metaphor from the writer of Hebrews, we do grow from spiritual babies, able to handle only the "milk" of the Spirit, to spiritual maturity, able to handle the real meat of the Spirit (Heb. 5:12–14). If every sheep in the flock entered in as fully grown, mature members of the flock, ministry would be an easy and a very fulfilling profession indeed. This, however, is the world after the fall. Things do not always work out so easily or neatly. The general principles stated throughout this book form the baseline for the shepherd's operation. But, we also want to give some ideas as to how a shepherd can more effectively reproduce leadership within his or her flock.

CREATING THE PROPER ENVIRONMENT

A leader is not truly great unless he or she reproduces more effective leaders. It does not matter how much a leader knows unless that leader possess the ability to pass it on. If a leader leaves and the church or business falls apart, then that leader was not at all successful, regardless of what actually occurred during the leader's tenure. Dale Galloway said it this way, "Only what we share multiplies."[1]

We are firm believers that the first step in multiplying the leaders of your flock is the environment. Is the atmosphere of your church or workplace conducive to people becoming leaders or wanting to explore leadership? For example, there are many things that a pastor in a normal, traditional church does—hospital visits, new membership follow-up, visitor follow-up, preaching, teaching, studying the Bible, discipling believers, and so on. If the shepherd is doing all of these things, where is the shared leadership? This is the issue of the pastor-centered church we just spoke of. How would the environment change if the pastor did only one or two of these tasks and allowed laity to lead the rest?

One tool a shepherd can use to create an environment of leadership is to start by looking at the specific areas where God has called that shepherd. In our experience, we know that Chris's strongest gifts lie in the areas of vision-casting, teaching/preaching, and leadership development. For Wayne it's counseling, pastoral care, and organization. We can both do other things, but we know those are our strengths. So, we begin to look at the areas of ministry needed outside the scope of our strengths and try to find laity who are gifted in those areas. This type of structure sends the signal that the shepherd is leading, but every part of the flock has an important role to play.

Another key aspect to creating a leadership-rich environment is for the shepherd to encourage existing leaders to constantly be looking for emerging leaders. As new blood is brought into positions of leadership two things occur. First, new ideas and energy are brought into the system. Second, as these new leaders are celebrated publicly the other sheep might think, "Hey, I know that guy.

He's just a normal person. Maybe that could be me someday." Thus the seeds for the next generation of leaders have been planted.

A final part to a healthy leadership environment is intentionality on the part of the shepherd. By intentionality we mean that expectations of the sheep-leaders are clearly outlined, proper training is given, and the core values of the church or organization are ingrained within these leaders. None of those steps happens by accident. Many sheep have a very knee-jerk reaction when asked to be in a position of leadership because they have no clue as to what they are supposed to do and they feel they will not be given the adequate training or direction to accomplish their task. No wonder they say no! A vital aspect of being a good shepherd is making sure your sheep-leaders have the resources to do what you ask of them.

The core values are the DNA of an organization. We have seen many cases where a church or business claims to have certain core values, but the reality of what is expressed by leadership is totally different. The "values" expressed may be the shepherd's core values, or they may be the ideal values, but they are not reality. When any living organism reproduces it passes its DNA on to its offspring. Through modern genetics it is possible to look at the DNA of a living human and tell where that person's ancestors lived. The same should be true of shepherds. The shepherd sets the core values for that flock. That DNA should be easily seen in all of the leaders of the flock whom the shepherd trains, as well as the leaders trained by the sheep-leaders. When everyone buys into the same system, then a ready supply of new leaders will always be available, and as they come online they will already be ingrained with the most important values of the flock. This is especially true of the core value of looking for new leadership.

IDENTIFICATION

If a positive environment of leadership exists, that is, if people are not shocked and, in fact, are excited when new leaders are found, then there must be a system for identifying those new leaders. The environment within the flock only creates an atmosphere where the sheep do not say "no" automatically when asked to be in a position of leadership. We feel that when the members of your flock know that they will not be blindsided by expectations, nor left to flounder on their own with no training, then they will say "yes" much more often.

How, then, do we identify these potential leaders? Every denomination and local church has their own method for selecting its leaders (for example, the nominating committee or the committee on committees). Within the church structure we often speak of spiritual gifts and use various tools and inventories to discover each member's gifts in an effort to best match each to his or her area of ministry. Getting your sheep plugged in to some type of service is a basic step that applies to all of them. Finding the leaders among the flock takes a little more work. Once persons begin working in their areas of ministry, they need to have a supervisor. This supervisor does not act as a boss, but as a resource person and source of encouragement. This one-on-one mentoring allows the leadership potential to be identified. The key is for the shepherd to train his or her supervisors to not only look at charismatic personalities, but also for results. Great leaders may be missed because they go about their business quietly, accomplishing great things from the background. People who are humble and not seeking self-aggrandizement may never have their leadership potential unlocked unless someone is working with them. Supervisors should be trained to look past the shell and see the attributes of leadership: creativity, resourcefulness, asking the right questions, dedication, constant learning, and production of results, to name a few. Personality may factor some into effective leadership, but it is not the only factor, nor even the most important, in our opinion. A strong introvert may turn out to be a very charismatic leader if given the right situation.

This point shows the next key step in identification of new leaders—recruiting. A healthy leadership environment may produce some people who volunteer for leadership, but the vast majority of potentially great leaders will have to be recruited. They may not even see themselves as leaders until someone else points out their potential. The best way for a shepherd to train the sheep-leaders in recruiting is to model it. Remind them, "You're here because I asked you. Who are you going to ask to step in to leadership?"

There is one point to keep in mind in recruiting: Know what your people are going to do. Do not simply recruit leaders for the sake of doing it. Have a mission in mind and know how to deploy them. Jon Cannon is a former Navy SEAL who wrote a book on leadership from the SEAL point of view. He noted that SEAL teams usually form two years in advance. When people are recruited to that SEAL team they don't know the exact mission they'll perform when they deploy two years down the road, but they know the basic types of missions they might have to perform and so plan, train, and recruit accordingly. Lt. Cmdr. Cannon writes, "Make sure you know what your people are going to be doing before you hire them. This doesn't mean you have to know the exact title and responsibility they'll have in two years. But you do need to know what personality traits and tool sets will be required. Then bring in only those people who have a chance of fitting into the role."[2] If you don't have a vision for your ministry you will not know how to successfully recruit those leaders who can help you succeed. Constantly ask yourself the question, "What leadership traits will I need to accomplish what God will call us to down the road?" Then recruit for the future rather than the past.

COACHING

The most effective way to train leaders and to ensure accountability, is, again, one-on-one. The shepherd does not have time to personally mentor every leader in his or her flock. Therefore, the wise shepherd will model mentoring to those in his or her "inner circle" and make clear the expectation that each leader be in a coaching relationship.

Ecclesiastes 4:12 states, "And though one might prevail against another, two will withstand one. A threefold cord is not quickly broken." This "threefold cord" mentality has been used in many leadership circles. The Promise Keepers movement brought the idea into the mainstream in the mid 1990s.[3] The basic concept is that every good leader has a mentor, is a mentor, and also maintains a relationship with an equal for accountability and encouragement. The shepherd who operates within the threefold cord principle will operate at maximum effectiveness. As the shepherd models this concept for the sheep, they will see its effectiveness and incorporate it into their own leadership habits.

The problem is that many shepherds only have one or two of the cords. They may have a coach and a close friend, or a student and a coach. All leaders need to learn from someone with more experience and wisdom than they have, and it is truly gratifying to be able to share your own wisdom and knowledge with someone else, but you also need a close friend who has no barriers with you—someone who is not accountable to you, nor you to them, in any official sense. This person can operate on equal footing with the shepherd, giving both encouragement and accountability as needed. This system will ensure that every leader in the flock is growing in competency and maintaining a healthy spiritual and emotional life.

Living into the Lesson

1. How intentional are you at picking your leaders?
2. Do you give your leaders freedom to mentor others? What are you intentionally doing to help raise up the "next generation" of leaders?
3. How intentional are you about recruiting your leadership? What can you do more effectively in this regard?

4. How effective are you at spotting people with relational authority? Have you placed others around you who know who the upcoming leaders are?
5. Have you intentionally made leadership reproduction a core value in your flock? What have you done effectively and what could you do better in conveying this core value?
6. Have you ever felt more like a sheep dog than a shepherd in your leadership? What situation caused these feelings? How did you handle the situation? What lessons did you learn?
7. What have you done to create an environment conducive to leadership in your flock? What could you do more effectively?
8. What system do you have in place for identifying potential leaders? How effective has this system been? What could you do to improve it?
9. Have you followed the threefold cord model: mentor, equal, and someone you coach? Which part do you need to add? How has this model helped your leadership?

9

CONCLUSION

Jesus said, "I have other sheep that do not belong to this fold" (John 10:16). This book has attempted to give the busy shepherd a means of understanding how and why certain sheep within their flock act and give some practical advice on how to most effectively lead those different types of sheep. We did not cover all the potential sheep in your flock. For example, there are Friday Sheep—the ones who are so focused elsewhere that they can't pay attention to what is actually happening in front of them. In modern psychobabble, these would be called "codependent." There are also many varieties of Wednesday Sheep, including some who will have a chronic mental or physical disorder. These rarer types of sheep require a lot of specialization and we have made no attempt to cover all possibilities.

This book has, however, covered the basic kinds of sheep the shepherd is most likely to find in each flock. This has been intended to be a practical guide for the busy shepherd. Those who wish to dig in to the research behind these observations are most welcome to do so. We have also included a few suggestions for more in-depth reading on specific, related subjects in our notes.

What we really hope the book has accomplished is to stimulate thinking about how you cannot lead every person in your flock in a "cookie-cutter" fashion. We hope we have given you some insight so that the next time you encounter one of these types of sheep in your flock you'll better understand how to lead them. We intentionally kept the book short and practically focused so that the busy shepherd (which means anyone in a leadership position) can find guidance for him- or herself and for the key people in the flock. Our hope is that this book will help you lead your sheep to become all that God created them to be.

One final word is in order. Early on we focused on basic listening and diagnostic skills. No matter how well these tools are applied, however, they will not be enough without one more—the skill of hospitality. Hospitality was a key virtue in biblical times. When three strangers came to Abram's tent on their way to Sodom, he showed them the best hospitality he could (Gen. 18). He did not know at the time that these men were really messengers on a mission from God. When Elijah came to Zarephath, a poor widow showed him the best hospitality she could (1 Kings 17). In Romans 12:13 Paul urged the church at Rome to show hospitality to both their church family and strangers. Peter took it one step further: "Be hospitable to one another without complaining" (1 Pet. 4:9).

From our own experience, and the biblical material, we know that hospitality means to make someone feel welcome. It means to make time and space in your busy life so that the other person can come into your life without feeling rushed and crowded. As we say here in the deep South, "Ya'll come on in and sit a spell."

To practice hospitality among the sheep means the shepherd (and the other leaders of the sheep) must have enough inner peace and calm that they can make room for the other sheep to tell their stories. It is in the telling of stories, both of success and defeat, that healing comes and relationships are built. To tell their stories the sheep must feel that their stories are welcome and that the shepherd, as much as they are, is being enriched by the stories. That is what happens among friends when they meet and fellowship. It is what must happen in the church if it is to truly be the church—those called to serve God's purposes.

A story about Martin Luther, a major figure in the Protestant Reformation, makes a great point. It is said that at the height of his work Luther prayed for about two hours each day. According to the story, someone asked him how he could afford to take two hours per day to pray when there were so many demands on his time—so many people to see, and books and letters to write. Luther replied, "I must pray two hours each day precisely because I am so busy." Whether that incident actually happened or not, it is great wisdom. Shepherds who are extremely busy need all the more to take time to pray, to calm their souls. Only then can they have the room in their busy lives to truly give hospitality to the sheep.

So listen to your sheep. Give them the oversight they need so they can find the green pastures and still waters. But don't neglect your own soul. Practice hospitality and let it begin with your own spiritual and relational life. Share with the sheep the calm you have found there. And may God richly bless you.

NOTES

INTRODUCTION

1. This is one of Maher's most widely circulated quotes from his *Politically Incorrect* show. It can be found quoted on many Internet sites, such as at http://thinkexist.com/quotation/we_need_more_people_speaking_out-this_country_is/330208.html.

2. See http://thinkexist.com/quotes/marilyn_manson/.

3. Cf. Revelation 7:17; Hebrews 13:20; 1 Peter 2:25.

CHAPTER 1

1. An excellent resource to explore these ideas further is Dr. Theodor Reik's book *Listening with the Third Ear* (New York: Farrar, Straus, and Giroux, 1983).

2. This is one of many great quotes on listening compiled by D. Tokay at Sabanci University; see http://www.sabanciuniv.edu.tr/bagem/writingcenter/eng/documents/pdfdocs/Fall_2004_Good_Listening_Skills_Quotes.pdf.

3. Taken from an October 15, 1888, letter Twain wrote to George Bainton, http://www.twainquotes.com/Lightning.html, accessed 4 December 2009.

4. Anthony Kenny, *Ancient Philosophy* (Oxford: Oxford University Press, 2007). Admittedly, however, there seems to be some discrepancy regarding the origin of this quote. A quick web search will show the attribution attached to everyone from Seneca to Buddha to Bob Dylan.

5. You can link to the VALS survey at http://www.strategicbusiness insights.com/vals/presurvey.shtml.

CHAPTER 2

1. For a thorough exploration of this subject we recommend John Maxwell's concept of the Level 5 leader. John Maxwell, *Developing the Leader within You* (Nashville: Thomas Nelson, 1993).

2. From "If 6 Was 9," The Jimi Hendrix Experience, *Axis: Bold as Love,* album released on Track Records in 1967.

3. George Barna, *The Second Coming of the Church* (Nashville: Word Publishing, 1998), 5.

CHAPTER 3

1. TA was first put forth by psychiatrist Eric Berne in the late 1950s. There are lots of good recent books on the subject, but Berne's classic is *Games People Play* (New York: Grove Press, 1964).

2. The book *Boundaries* by Dr. Henry Cloud and Dr. John Townsend is an excellent read for any leader (Grand Rapids: Zondervan, 1992).

3. C. Wayne Perry, "First look: what brings clergy candidates into ministry and what happens when they don't get it," *The Journal for Pastoral Care* 57/1 (2003): 15–25.

CHAPTER 4

1. John Phillips, "Monday, Monday" on *If You Can Believe Your Eyes and Ears,* recorded by The Mamas and the Papas, Dunhill Records, 1966.

2. Jonathan Edwards, "Sinners in the Hands of an Angry God," sermon, Enfield, Conn., 8 July 1741.

3. R. C. Kessler, W. T. Chu, O. Dennier, and E. E. Walters, "Prevalence, severity, and comorbidity of twelve month DSMIV disorders in the National Comorbidity Survey Replication (NCSR), *Archives of General Psychiatry* 62/6 (2005): 617–27.

4. Howard H. Goldman et al., eds., *Mental Illness: A Report of the Surgeon General,* chapter 2, "The fundamentals of Mental Health and

Mental Illness," in the section "Overview of Treartment," http://www.surgeongeneral.gov/library/mentalhealth/chapter2/sec6.html, accessed 15 December 2009.

CHAPTER 5

1. Selima Ben Mansour, Elyes Jouini, and Clotilde Napp, "Is There a Pessimistic Bias in Individual Beliefs? Evidence from a Simple Survey," Social Science Research Network (July 7, 2006), http://ssrn.com/abstract=915382, accessed December 4, 2009. This paper is one of many examples that show the bias of women being more pessimistic than men.

2. C. S. Lewis, *The Great Divorce* (New York: Harper One, 2001).

CHAPTER 6

1. We have not been able to verify the origination of this quote. It seems to be most often attributed to either author Oscar Wilde or Alice Roosevelt Longworth, daughter of President Teddy Roosevelt.

2. Deuteronomy 6:5 and Leviticus 19:18, respectively.

3. Matthew 22:37–40.

4. From Tillich's most famous sermon, "You Are Accepted," which was eventually published as chapter 19 in *The Shaking of the Foundations* (New York: Charles Scribner's Sons, 1955). The book is currently out of print, but the sermon is viewable online at http://www.religion-online.org/showchapter.asp?title=378&C=84.

5. C. Wayne Perry, "First look: what brings clergy candidates into ministry and what happens when they don't get it," *The Journal For Pastoral Care* 57, no. 1 (2003).

6. Exodus 4:10, 1 Samuel 9–10, and Jeremiah 20:7–10, respectively.

7. American Psychiatric Association, *Diagnostic and Statistical Manual of Mental Disorders*, 4th ed. (Washington, D.C.: American Psychiatric Publishing, 1994).

CHAPTER 7

1. American Psychiatric Association, *Diagnostic and Statistical Manual of Mental Disorders*, 4th ed., text revision (DSM-IV-TR) (Arlington, Va.: American Psychiatric Association, 2000).

2. Ibid.

CHAPTER 8

1. Dale Galloway, class lecture, Asbury Theological Seminary, Nov. 4, 2003.

2. Jeff Cannon and Lt. Cmdr. Jon Cannon, *Leadership Lessons of the Navy SEALS* (New York: McGraw-Hill, 2003).

3. Bill McCartney et al., *Seven Promises of a Promise Keeper* (Nashville: Thomas Nelson, 1999).